Til

Astrology

Ancient Tibetan Wisdom to Lighten Our Path of Progress and Guide Our Future

Tsering Dolma Drungtso

Drungtso Publications

Tibetan Elemental Astrology

(Ancient Tibetan Wisdom to Lighten Our Path of Progress and Guide Our Future)

Copyright © Drungtso Publications 2002
First Published in 2002 by Drungtso Publications
Printed at Indraprastha Press (CBT), New Delhi.

Cover art & Drawing by: Tenzin Dawa

Drungtso Publications
C/O Men Tsee Khang College, Gangchen Kyishong, Dharamsala-176215, H.P. (India)
Tel: 01892-28034 (Res.)
Handy: 9817092550
Email: drdrungtso@yahoo.com
tibastro@yahoo.com

ISBN: 81-901395-0-9   Price: Rs. 350/-

*Tsering Dolma Drungtso while conducting course
on Tibetan Astrology*

CONTENTS

iv

AUTHOR'S PREFACE

Tibetan Astrology is worth mentioning to consult for our life guidance. By doing so, we can avoid obstacles, misfortune, wrong career, wrong decisions, and painful mistakes. The ancient wisdom of Tibetan astrology can be used from the ground level activities like to see a good date for opening a shop, restaurant, marriage ceremony, to a greater activities like political meeting, and religious practices. There are three major sections in Tibetan astrology which are, Elemental astrology, Astronomy and Tibetan astrology of Arising vowels. This book is meant for the beginner student and mainly deals with the Elemental astrological knowledge. I have done my very best to present this knowledge in a simple, informative and comprehensive format to meet your needs.

The information provided in this handy book is an authentic source for those who wish to develop one's astrological knowledge. It is mainly based on the teachings of my late teacher, Prof. Drakton and the authentic elemental astrological text, Moon Rays Oral Instruction Elemental ('byung rtsis man ngag zla bai 'od zer).

This handy book can be used profitably by anyone interested in developing one's Astro. Knowledge. I hope this book will prove useful and satisfying for everyone.

DEDICATION

I dedicate this work to my respected teacher, the late Professor Jampa Gyaltsen Drakthon (1939–1997) who trained me with great kindness and answered and cleared my countless doubts. Professor Jampa Gyaltsen Drakthon, was recognised as the most learned scholar with profound knowledge in all the ten fields of study (rig gnas bcu). He served as the Director of Astrology for over thirty years at T.M.A.I (Tibetan Medical & Astro. Institute of H.H. the Dalai Lama).

May the stars, planets, sun and moon guide his soul to love, peace, vitality and happiness forever.

ACKNOWLEDGMENTS

To my respected teacher, the late Prof. Jampa Gyaltsen Dakthon for his instruction and blessing.

To my beloved husband Dr. Tsering Thakchoe Drungtso, for his unfailing encouragement and support for my work.

To my brother, Tenzin Dawa, for writing the cover design and arts.

To Mr. Tenzin Rabten, a competent computer master for his assistance in cover art designing and texts setting.

To all others not mentioned, for their help and support.

FOREWORD

By Dr. Tsering Thakchoe Drungtso

Tibetan Elemental Astrology by Tsering Dolma Drungtso is a reliable method of life guidance based on the time tested ancient Tibetan wisdom. Humans have for centuries lived within the flow of nature. However, modern life-styles have twisted our peaceful existence into one of the chaos and extremes, resulting in ending in disharmony and disastrous results for the inhabitants. Concerning the elements, the Four Classic Treatise of Tibetan Medicine states:

All living and non living beings are formed by the five elements. The sustenance and harmony as well as all the sickness, disharmony and destruction are due to elements. The antidotes of the sickness and destruction are also five elements in origin and composition. Therefore, all the three (formation, sustenance and destruction) are interrelated for having common origin of the five elements (Earth, Water, Fire, Air and Space). Prevention is always better than cure, so the saying goes. Astrology enables us to understand this aspect to promote prosperity, harmony and vitality as well as tune into a person's beneficial position, thereby helps in preventing sickness and worldly disaster.

Tibetan Healing Science and Astrology are closely related and are found from the same elemental root. The different comes from the mode of application. Tibetan Medicine works more on the physical level, whereas Tibetan Astrology works more on the psychological and mental ground.

Astrology in general has no barrier with religious belief, caste, nationality etc., and can be used beneficially by every one. It is as important as our environment, which is closely related with every one of us. Therefore, the biased view placed upon astrology as superstition and folklore can be removed by through study at this science. This science's roots are traceable to the experiments done by our ancestors. Even at this moment we notice, the influence of the environment, nature, elements, earth's gravity, electromagnetic fields and constellations etc., on our actions and well being. Thus it is clear that astrological science can be explained by logic.

The instructions given in the book will create a bond with you to know exactly who you are, what you want and to whom you associate. It gives tips on how to choose one's best life-partner, business partner and tells secrets of knowing other's personalities as well. However, it is important to keep in mind that, astrology cannot reveal all the information about someone. The reason is simple, because there are many factors (causes, circumstances, karma and law of cause and effect etc.,) which influence the course of an individuals life. Khedrub Jey, a greater Tibetan master in a commentary on Kalachakra Tantra stated; if astrology reveals all the information about an individual, then a human being and a dog born in the same place and at the same time would have the same characteristics, the same nature, the same life-span, and the same things happen to them during their lifetime. When we really go deep inside this subject, it will take us to the idea of reincarnations, and how one can understand so many mysteries of life such as irrational fears, destructive relationships, feelings of familiarity, deeply rooted habit patterns, and skills that seem to come so naturally etc. This is the depth and vast of the subject.

This handy book by Dolma is designed to help you find out and takes the reader on an exciting adventure of exploration and discovery by which one understand one's root being.

This book is written in simple instructions and contains calculations on various subjects offering a unique system of self-discovery. The author recognizes that astrology shows us not only the roots of our behavior, our response to stress, our survival instincts and our ambitions but also our potential to achieve fulfillment and reach our goals in life. If one can take a little serious study on the subject of the book one can apply it to oneself and others with considerable benefit. The planets, elements, animal signs, constellations, I-Chings, Magic square numbers, etc. indicate what sort of nature a person possesses and the type of means he/she should adopt for attaining progress, happiness, health and achievement in one's life. The attainment of spiritual salvation and benefit of life is possible only by practicing a certain way of life as indicated in one's life horoscope by professional and learned astrologers. The life horoscope reveals one's past lives, present life and next birth. I am sure this simple and informative book on Tibetan Elemental Astrology, based on the knowledge derived from the great Tibetan scholars and masters, authentic texts and author's own experience as a professional astrological and Feng Shui consultant will definitely offer fine solutions to the problems all of us face. It is worth mentioning that this small booklet is highly standard and reliable. If you really want to know the ongoing of your life, the ocean of valuable life guidance will find within the pages of this book. The author discuss the work which you are best suited, pinpoint your special talents, etc. Understanding this ancient wisdom of Tibet, offers you the power to change and transforms your challenges into opportunities. This book is meant to be used, not simply read.

Dolma's work proves to be extremely informative and I

should say this is an excellent contribution for the promotion of Tibetan astrology beyond the boundary.

Drungtso publishers is highly honoured and privileged to host and bring the publication of this book to provides valuable guide and reference for readers to determine the important aspects of human life, marriage, children, profession, finance, carrier, etc. It is our hope that this book will encourage wider readership and facilitate further interest on Tibetan astrology.

Dr. Tsering Thakchoe Drungtso (Lecturer)
1st of January 2002.
(TIBETAN MEDICAL & ASTROLOGICAL COLLEGE OF H.H. THE DALAI LAMA, DHARAMSALA)

Dr. Tsering Thakchoe Drungtso is author of Tibetan Medicine -The Healing Science of Tibet and co-author of Tibetan English Dictionary of Tibetan Medicine and Astrology. He had been the advisor for several books on Tibetan Medicine such as Developing the Art of Tibetan Medicine by Noah DeGaetano, USA and Treatment of Srog-rLung without Golden Needle by Eveleyens, Holland.

He had also been an advisor of Tibetan Medical and Astrological College Magazine Gangri-Langtso (English section) since 1998 and still holds the same responsibility. He had translated from English to Tibetan, several medical research papers, and more recently the book, *Eye care in Developing Nations*. At present Dr. Drungtso holds the position of lecturer at the Tibetan Medical and Astrological College, Dharamsala. Dr. Drungtso is one of the best English-speaking teachers on Tibetan Medicine and he had students from USA, Germany, Holland, Swiss, Spain, Japan and Austria.

"Three decades of days make a month, when twelve of these pass we have a year. When seven hundred and twenty pass, of days and nights, we have three hundred and sixty 'days', when these pass we have a year. The days are divided in male and female. Autumn, spring, summer and winter have threemonths each. In relation to the five elements and the twelve animals: mouse, ox, tiger, rabbit, dragon, snake, horse, sheep, monkey, bird, dog and pig, are unfolded the astrological calculations of the elements."

Prof. Namkahi Norbu Rinpoche

History and Origin of Tibetan Astro. Science

Tibet was one of the equal standing nations like that of our neighbouring countries such as China and India with distinct culture, history and language. The Tibetan system of Astrology is a comprehensive science still practiced in Tibet as well as within the Buddhist cycle. Though Tibetan Astrology shares similarities with Indian Astrology and the Chinese system of astrology, it is its own unique system based on the culture and tradition of Tibet. The Tibetan system of Astrology is the unification of all the essence lore of astrology from neighbouring countries such as Kalachakra Astrology from India and the Chinese system of Elemental astrology. However, Tibet had a rudimentary system of Astrology based primary on the Bon Tradition and ancient culture of Tibet before the advent of Buddhism.

This science is classified into three categories. There are: Astronomy (sKar rtsis), Elemental Astrology ('byung rtsis) and Shiva Sarvodaya Tantra (byang 'char). Some scholars are not aware of the ancient Tibetan Astrological science, and they think that there was no knowledge on Tibetan astrology and astronomy in Tibet before 3rd century and earlier to the King Nyatri Tsenpo. This

1

wrong belief distorts the real history of ancient Tibetan astrology. So I would like to clarify this wrong belief and notion about the history of Tibetan Astrological science by narrating what the history tell us about the sequence of development in Tibetan Astrology. Since the earliest period of time, going back at least 3000 years, people had discovered the natural force of elements and they had a time during which they worshiped the nature: fire, water, mountain, lakes, forest, the sun and the moon etc. Thus, I do believe that, the Tibetan astrology had been grown up from it's root since then.

The most complete system of Elemental Astrology was believed to be originated from China. It is believed that it was first expounded in the Wood-Mouse year (836 B.C.) by Manjushri in a place called the five mountain peaks (Ribo rtse lnga). He had many disciples; sixteen being outstanding ones out of whom following four excellent disciples Brahamin Ser-kya (Tib.Bram-ze Ser-kya), Ushnishavijaya (Tib. Lhamo rNamgyal-ma), Brahama (Tib. Lhachen Tsangpa), Nagaraja Taksaka (Tib. Klu-rgyal 'jog-po) requested for following teachings.

1) Bram-ze Ser-kya (Brahamin Ser-kya), asked for Kek rtsis (Yearly horoscope). This subject deals with the yearly prognostication regarding health, wealth, and positive and negative happinings of the particular year.

2) Lhamo rNamgyal-ma (Ushnishavijaya), asked for Bag rtsis (Marital Astrology). This subject deals with the compatibility of persons for marriage.

3) Lhachen Tsangpa (Brahama), asked for Gshin rtsis (Death Astrology). This subject deals with the calculations to be made after the death of a person.

4) Klu-rgyal 'jog-po (Nagaraja Taksaka), asked for Tshe-rab las-rtsis (Natal horoscope). This subject deals with the prognostication regarding the whole life happenings of a person.

According to legend the mythical emperor Fu Hshi (Tib. sPa-Hu- hshi-dhi), saw a golden coloured turtle that was offered to him by a subject from the coastal region, and upon inspecting it the patterns of the eight Parkha first arose in his mind. Based on the inspection made upon this, the Astrology system with respect to the eight trigrams (parkha), the nine magic square number (sMeba) and the twelve animal signs were devised. Later the king, ministers and learned scholars who had mastered these techniques composed astrological treatises.

Particularly Confucius, who was an emanation of Manjushri and who is known in Tibetan under the name "Kongtse Phrul rgyal", introduced treatises on Astrology where the details of rituals and divinations are extensively expounded.

It is believed that the five elements are the gifts of Lord Manjushri. Here comes the explanation of how elements came into being. The story goes during the gloomy period, when there was nothing other than the existence of the clear space in this universe (Space element). Space and Iron element share common characteristic of stability. It was during that time, Lord Manjushri from his celestial region blow an air from his nose and created the wind cycle in our universe. Wind is closely related with trees (Wood element) with the common characteristic of movement. The spittle fall from the Manjushri's tongue finally changed into seas and oceans (Water element). Upon that, the Earth cycle was formed by his power of sight (Earth element). After that appears the Fire cycle from the burning intellect sword of Manjushri (Fire element). This is the story how cycles of elements are offered by Lord Manjushri. There is also other legendary tale how Manjushri taught the elemental astrology through five kinds of his emanated Golden tortoises.

At the time of the first King, Nyatri Tsenpo (1136 B.C.), there exist twelve major teachings of Bon tradition (rGyui' *Bon shespa can bcu gnyis*). Among which Koe-she Tsee-khan is the name of one astrological text which derived its name from an expert Bon astrologer (Tib.

skos shes rtsis mkhan), who knows not only movement of the sun, moon and constellation but also check the seasons and guides the farmers and nomads. Tibetan culture such as medicine and Astrology were well existed since then. The tradition of incense burning ceremony, performing ransom and cross thread rituals which are still practice today has its root in the Ancient Tibetan civilization.

During the reign of 33rd King Songtsen Gampo (617-650 A.D.), his Chinese wife Kongjo has brought many books on Elemental Astrology which leads to the further development of Tibetan Astro. Science. Therefore, earlier Astrological knowledge based on the principles of Zhang zhung culture was influenced by Chinese classical elemental Astrology and made a complete shape to it.

The astro. Texts which Kongjo brought to Tibet includes 'byung ba rinchen kun 'dus (jung wa rinchen kundue), Sel sgron sbas bcad med pa (sel don bey chey me pa), Rinchen sungs pa (rinchen sungpa), sdong po kun 'dus (dongpo kundue), spor thang brgyad cu'i dpe ris (porthang geychue pey ree)-the eighty hidden astrology etc. and well progressed the Tibetan system of astronomy. She was not only expert in examined the eighty hidden astrology but also well experienced in Feng shui (Geomancy). During this period, four Tibetan Scholar were sent to China to study Astrology. They studied rtis gzhung lugs rgyud sde dgu (tsee shung look gyue de goo), 'brel pa gsum (delpa soom), rus sbal gyi gab rtse dpe ris (rue bel gee gabze pe ree). Lopon 'Barba Chom-chom had translated these texts into Tibetan from Chinese origin.

"Thus the Bon and Buddhist astrological principles were influenced by Chinese classical Elemental Astrology, as well as by Astrological principles from several neighbouring countries such as India and even Persia and Greece."

—(Late) Prof. Jampa Gyaltsen Drakthon

What is Tibetan Elemental Astrology?

Tibetan Elemental Astrology, byung-rTsis is also known as Nag rtsis which means black calculation. Elemental astrology is considered to have originated in China.

This system deals mainly with the calculation of five elements viz. Wood, Fire, Earth, Metal and Water in relation with the twelve animal signs, eight trigrams (parkha), nine magic square number (sMeba). Each year has its own element and animal sign, and also each month, day and hour has its own element and the sign.

Tibetan Astrologer examines the five sectors of life very importantly in the elemental calculation: 1) Srog-one's life force, 2) Lus-Body/health, 3) dbang thang-power or financial status, 4) klung rta-luck/success in one's work and 5) bla-life soul.

Elemental Astrology is used to construct the five major areas.

1) Yearly Prediction (keg rtsis):
It forecasts the happenings in each year and will indicate if there will be any financial, health or work problem. The Astrologer can also give remedial measures in order to avoid obstacles.

2) Natal horoscope (tse-rab- le-rtsis):
It reveals one's information about astrological deity, past life and next life. The main purpose of Tibetan astro. chart is to alert one during the definite wrathful and unfavourable period as well as guide one to follow any important carrier or job on a specified good day. Ritual and remedies will be given where there is needed to avoid and overcome hindrances and bad luck.

3) Marriage compatibility Chart (Bag rtsis):
It deals with the marriage and taken considerably importance in the Tibetan society for a couple to ensure a happy and successful life with one's life partner. The astrologer can advise which animals signs will be the best suited and pick up favourable date and time to get wedding ceremony. Whereas if the astrologer find disharmony between partners, but if the partners have strong desire to get marry, then the astrologer will prescribe remedial measure or antidotes to bring happiness and avoid hindrance.

4) Medical Astrology (Nad rtsis):
Tibetan astrologer prepares a medical chart for those who did not get cure despite their consultant to high and fame doctors and lengthy intake of medicines. For this case the Astrologer will give advice as to which doctor

or system of medicine is the most suitable. There are certain diseases caused by past karma and certain maladies which are due to the effect of evil spirits. This can be determined through astro. Knowledge. The astrologer can specify which spirits are afflicting the sick person. Appropriate special prayers and rituals are prescribed by the astrologer to please the evil spirits, withoutwhich mere medication will not be possible to eliminate the hindrance and sickness caused by evil spirits.

5) Death Calculation (gshin rtsis):
According to the Tibetan tradition, when a person dies, it is very important for the family of the deceased to ask an astrologer or to a high lama to cast a death calculation. The astrologer needs to know the dead person's date and time of birth and the number of family members the deceased had at the time death and their animals signs. From this, they can find an auspicious day for the disposal of the body and can advise whether any special ritual needs to be performed to prevent any misfortunes befalling the rest of the family. Those people with incompatible animal signs should not be allowed to touch or see the dead body. The colour of cloth that covers the face of the deceased should be given.

"One can experience the sacred in oneself in relation to these elements through connecting, or experiencing, or being. The shamans connect with nature. The Tantric practitioner experiences energy, and the dzogchen practitioner experiences a quality of abiding in the five pure lights and five pure presences."

—***Tenzin Wangyal Rinpoche***

Introduction to the Five Elements

The five elements theory states that all physical phenomena, whether in the macrocosms or microcosmic world, are formed by the five energies of Wood, Fire, Earth, Metal and Water. The five elements play a major role in the Elemental Astrology and is used with almost every calculation. The elements are explained fully under the five subjects as shown below:

1) The nature of the elements- (Ngo-bo)
2) Significance of the elements- (Nges- tshig)
3) Classification-(dBye-ba)
4) Characteristic of the elements-(mTshan nyid)
5) The functions-(byed-las).

The nature of the elements:
The Moon Rays Oral Instruction Elemental Text states: The nature of the elements is that when the elements are investigated, they no longer exist as an external matter due to its extreme subtlety (Tib. brtag na dben phyir ma grub ste).

Significance of the elements:
Since we lack the subtle wisdom to understand the true

subtle nature of elements, it is best to define that the five Elements emerged naturally on this earth.

Classification of the elements:
It has five aspects (Wood, Fire, Earth, Metal, Water) and seven or eight when space (mkha'), mountain (ri) and air (rlung) are added.

Characteristic of the elements:
The characteristics of the five elements are:
Wood-Mobility, Fire-Burn, Earth-Solidity, Metal-Cutting and Water-Fluidity.

Functions of the elements:
When the functions of the elements are not disturbed, one will enjoy good health and gain happiness. Whereas, when the functions of the elements are disturbed, then it will give rise to sickness, suffering and may leads to death.

Therefore the body which is an aggregate of these elements is influenced by three humoral disorders, primordial bewitchers, and the four adversarial signs, which are all originally derive from ignorance. Elements are responsible for all the happiness and suffering.

The elements have three types of applications: Internal,

External and Alternative. The external elements are Wood (shing), Fire (me), Earth (sa), Metal (lcag) and Water (chu).

The elements appear Internally as nerves and muscle (Wood), digestive heat (Fire), flesh (Earth), bone (Metal) and blood (Water).

The alternative elements correspond to the five vital and six hollow organs: Liver and gall bladder (Wood), heart and small intestine (Fire), spleen and stomach (Earth), lungs and large intestine (Metal) and the kidneys, seminal vesicle and urinary bladder (Water).

"For Shamans the earth is sacred earth, water is sacred water, fire is sacred fire, air is sacred air, space is sacred space. In Shamanism, working with the raw natural elements involves connecting with the external element and internalizing its qualities at deeper and deeper levels, until one ultimately connects with the very essence of the element."
—Tenzin Wangyal Rinpoche

Table no.1
Details of the elements

External Element	Internal Element	Alternative Element	Symbol	Season	Color	Planet	Direction
Wood	Liver	Nerves & Muscles	Rectangle	Spring	Green	Jupiter	East
Fire	Heart	Heat	Triangle	Summer	Red	Sun, Mars	South
Earth	Spleen	Flesh	Square	Inter-season	Yellow	Saturn	Cardinal
Metal	Lungs	Bone	Semi- Circle	Autumn	White	Venus	West
Water	Kidneys	Blood	Circle	Winter	Blue/ Black	Moon, Mercury	North

Recognition of Bone Element (Rus-khams)

In the early day people were familiar about their bone element and could tell their own bone element (Rus khams) without any difficulties. With the passage of time, the practice of knowing one's bone element came to an end. So, today, most of the people can not tell their own bone element. Therefore, I explain here how to recognize one's bone element. To understand your bone element, you must use your birth sMeba and connect it with the bone element.

Let's say, if your birth sMeba is Green "4" and it is related with the wood element. Therefore you bone element (Rus khams) would be Keg. It is fixed with birth sMeba element.

One can also recognize the bone element (Rus khams) from the characteristic of the person.

The five bone element (Rus khams) are Keg (Wood), Ji (Fire), Kung (Earth), Shang (Metal), Vu (Water).

Keg: These person are characterised by hoarseness, speak from the throat with stammering (skad 'gags gre ba 'dar keg shing).

Ji: Their speech or voice usually comes through the teeth (so bar sgra 'don ji me ste).

Kung: They have habit of inhaling deep from the naval part while speaking (lte khung dbugs sdud kungs sa dang)

Shang: These person has a habbit of speaking with a mouth wide open, a tongue often hangs outside and breathes noisily while speaking (kha gdangs lche 'phyar sna nas dbugs 'ong ba de ni gshang lchags khams).

Vu: They frequently open and close their lips while speaking (chu bsdud chu 'zum vu chu bshad).

Table no. 2
Rus khams

Birth sMeba	4	7,9	5	1,6,8	2,3
Elements	Wood	Fire	Earth	Metal	Water
Rus Kham	Keg	Ji	Kung	Shang	Vu

"Since the 2nd century B.C., Elemental Astrology was in wide use, and it remained close to the Bon tradition for hundreds of years."
— *(Late) Prof. Jampa Gyaltsen Drakthon*

Elemental Relationships

The relationship of the elements mother and child, foe and friend are mostly calculated through the compatibility and incompatibility between the elements.

The calculation of the four processes of the elemental relationship:

Use your left hand and place the five elements in the following places:

Wood-on thumb

Fire-on forefinger

Earth-on middle finger

Metal-on ring finger

Water-on little finger.

Figure 1A: Respective place of elements

The process of mother relationship

To find the mother relationship, you should always work in an upward direction. Example: Wood-mother-Water. The mother of Wood is Water because we all know that Wood can grow with the help of Water. The mother of Water is Metal because the origin of Water element is from Metal. You might have known that when we heat Metal at a certain temperature, Water is produced. The mother of Metal is Earth. One can learn the origin of the mineral from this relationship as Metal is hidden deep inside the Earth. Earth acts as a major contributor to keeping the mineral (Metal) deep inside it for hundreds of thousands of years providing the optimum temperature for them to carry out the process of evaporation and other chemical reactions of the different substances to compose the new mineral. The mother of Earth is Fire as Earth is the ash product of the Fire. The mother of Fire is Wood, without Wood there is no Fire.

The mother of Wood is WATER
The mother of Water is METAL
The mother of Metal is EARTH
The mother of Earth is FIRE
The mother of Fire is WOOD

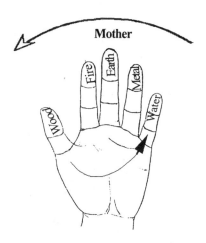

Figure 1B: Mother Relationship

WOOD→WATER→ METAL→EARTH→FIRE

The process of child relationship:

To find the child relationship, work in the opposite direction of the mother relationship i.e. work in a downward direction.

The child of Wood is Fire because burning wood creates Fire. The child of Fire is Earth as Fire leaves Earth. The child of Earth is Metal because Earth creates Metal. The child of Metal is Water that Metal liquefies. The child of Water is Wood because Water nurtures plants (Wood).

19

The child of Wood is FIRE
The child of Fire is EARTH
The child of Earth is METAL
The child of Metal is WATER
The child of Water is WOOD

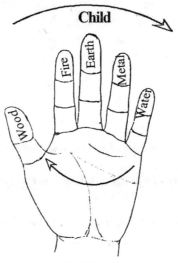

Figure 1C: Child Relationship

WOOD→FIRE→EARTH→ METAL→WATER

The process of enemy relationship:

The enemy of Wood is Metal as a Metal instrument, such as an axe, can cut down the trees (Wood). The enemy of Metal is Fire because Fire melts down Metal. The enemy of Fire is Water, as Water will extinguish Fire. The enemy of Water is Earth; the Earth element absorbs water. The enemy of Earth is Wood; wood grows at the expense of impoverishing Earth.

Always start from the thumb (wood element) and skip two fingers. The next element is the enemy of the Wood element. Then again skip two fingers and the next element will be the enemy of Metal that is Fire.

The enemy of Wood is METAL
The enemy of Metal is FIRE
The enemy of Fire is WATER
The enemy of Water is EARTH
The enemy of Earth is WOOD.

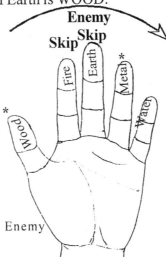

Figure 1D: Enemy
Relationship

WOOD → METAL → FIRE → WATER → EARTH

The process of friend relationship:

The friend of Wood is Earth. Wood can grow with the help of Earth. The friend of Earth is Water. Both the Earth and Water combine to help the inhabitants of the Earth carry out their existence. The friend of Water is Fire. The Fire element gives warmth to the Water. The friend of Fire is Metal as it helps to increase the strength of Fire. The friend of Metal is Wood because it supplies the handle to the weapons (Metal).

To find the elemental friend relationship, we have to know what friendship means getting help and assisting each other. First you start from the thumb (Wood element) and skip one finger. The next element is the friend of Wood. Again skip one finger and so on.

The friend of Wood is EARTH
The friend of Earth is WATER
The friend of Water is FIRE
The friend of Fire is METAL
The friend of Metal is WOOD

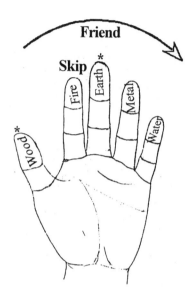

Figure 1C: Friend Relationship

WOOD→EARTH→WATER→FIRE→METAL

23

Table no. 3
Elemental Relationship (Ma, Bu, Da, Dok)

Self	WOOD	FIRE	EARTH	METAL	WATER
Mother	Water	Wood	Fire	Earth	Metal
Child	Fire	Earth	Metal	Water	Wood
Friend	Earth	Metal	Water	Wood	Fire
Foe	Metal	Water	Wood	Fire	Earth

Table no. 4
Medical System of Ma, Bu, Da, Dok
(Elemental Relationship)

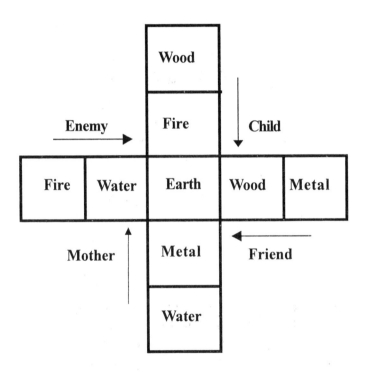

Table no. 4
Chinese System of Ma, Bu, Da, Dok
(elemental relationship)

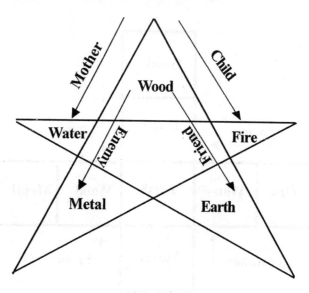

"The practitioners of Tibet's ancient Bon religion had acknowledged the five elements many years earlier, and used a system of astrological prediction and divination, which was similar to shamanism with its techniques of black and white magic and animal sacrifice."

-Prof. Jampa Gyaltsen Drakthon (Late)-

The Twelve Animal Signs

The twelve animal signs are Mouse (byi ba), Ox (gLang), Tiger (sTag), Rabbit (Yos), Dragon ('brug), Snake (sBrul), Horse (rTa), Sheep (Lug), Monkey (sPrel), Bird (bya), Dog (Khyi) and Pig (phag).

They can be classified into two groups: Male and Female. The first in the animal sign cycle is always male year, whereas the next to it becomes female year. Each of the twelve animal signs correlate in turn to one of the five elements, Wood, Fire, Earth, Metal and Water. One can easily find out the year of an individual by knowing the person's animal sign along with one of the five elements.

These twelve animal signs are classified into two groups: Antagonism and Harmony. So, one should find or avoid the unfavourable sign before one get married. The connection between animals can be favorable or unfavourable. An understanding of their affinities is important when human relationships are under consideration-partnerships, marriages, friendships etc.

The Characteristic of the Twelve Animal Signs:

Animal sign: Mouse

Year: 1996, 1984, 1972, 1960, 1948, 1936, 1924, 1912 and 1900

Personality:

A person born in the year of Mouse is curious, intellectual and hard working. They reach everywhere. They are also sharp minded and creative by nature. But they are a bit careless in most of the work they undertake and can be selfish. They are able to save a great deal of money because of their stingy nature. Most of these people are good in their studies. They are jolly and easily make friends. They are smily and lovely person. They are experts in house- hold life and are tactful. Honest, ambitious, charming, quick to anger, gossipy and energetic. They get along easily with others and adapt themselves very well to changing environments and are experts in ingratiating to others. They are gentle and loving by nature.

Suitable Occupations: Business, Writer
Favourable partner: Dragon, Monkey
Unfavourable partner: Horse, Rabbit, Bird, Tiger and Dog
Famous people had born in this sign: H.H. Sixteenth Gyalwa Karmapa, Shungsep Jetsun (Tibetan Yogini), Rakra Rinpoche, Dr. Tenzin Choedrak (Senior personal physician to H.H. The 14th Dalai Lama), Galileo, Leo Tolstoy,Washington, Shakespeare.

Animal Sign: Ox
Year: 1997, 1985, 1973, 1961, 1949, 1937, 1925, 1913, and 1901
Personality:
People born in the ox year are loyal and diligent. They are honest, ambitious, intelligent and sharp minded. They are capable leaders and often receive encouragement and complements from others. They are introverted calm, obedient and outwardly gentle, though have a lot of

pride. Diplomacy and using preliminary steps are always in their mind while doing any major task. They are hard working, responsible and never leave their work incomplete. They are patient, easy going, confident but often narrow minded and stubborn. Talks little, feel shyness; love to complete their work on time. Affectionate by nature, delay in marriage, tolerant, excellent leader and demand as much from themselves as of other. They are strong, solid and enjoy good health. They are honest, stable and do not change their mind easily. Slow but good steady worker. The ox is also strong-headed and prefers to act alone. They are sincere, reliable, reserved and trustworthy. Most of them are intellectual and constantly in love. They may become furious and violent when severely angered. They are not afraid of hardship, do not give up easily and are steadfast in their thinking. Besides being conservative, they are also one who abides by rules. They do not make romantic wives and husbands. These people are well disciplined and expert in controlling others. They are independent and prefer to stand in their own two feet. They enjoy eating and sleeping.

Suitable Occupations: Surgery, Medical profession, Chief army, Beautician

Favourable partner: Snake, Bird

Unfavourable partner: Sheep, Dog, Dragon, Pig and

Rabbit

Famous people had born in this sign: H.H. Seventeenth Gyalwa Karmapa, Dubthob Thangtong Gyalpo (Chaksampa), Late Khyabje Yongdzin Trijang Rinpoche, Prof. Dawa Norbu, Napoleon, Richard Nixon, Jawaharla Nehru, Napoleon Bonaparte, Adolf Hitler.

Animal sign: Tiger
Year: 1998, 1986, 1974, 1962, 1950, 1938, 1926, 1914, 1902, and 1890
Personality:
Those born in the Tiger year are exceptionally self-confident, very possessive, forceful, impulsive and have a strong sense of superiority over others. They are physically and mentally active, and are sympathetic but a bit arrogant and proud. These people are brave, endeavour, career-minded and intelligent by nature. They are friendly with others but hate gossiping. They can

summount most obstacles, think a lot, and are inclined to be a bit jealous. They have a forceful personality and are ambitious, believing that no one is better or braver. They will occasionally use harsh words when speaking with others. They are bold and patient and will able to face hardships in life. They are helpful to mankind and strong willed. They usually prefer to stay alone but have a strong affection for their relatives. They are good natured, frank, outspoken, very independent in views and have excellent organization skills. They are ambitious, generous, determined, honourable, warm hearted, self-confident, fearless and fond of power and destructions, large hearted and noble but harsh temperament. They are brave, have a fighting spirit, sensitive, deep thinkers and stubbornly courageous. They hardly trust others and are hard working person. These people are very intelligent, love playing or entertaining, kind towards kids, changeable by nature, clever, stable minded and honest by nature. They are also quite self-centered and like to do things their own way. They possesses an adventurous spirit and the ability to overcome obstacles.

Suitable Occupations: Social work, Racer, Leader, Driver

Favourable partner: Horse, Dog

Unfavourable partner: Monkey, Snake, Pig, Dragon and Mouse

Famous people had born in this sign: Panchen Choe-kyi Gyaltsen (10th Panchen Lama), Sakya Pandita Kunga Gyaltsen, Lobpon Tenzin Namdak, Sogyal Rinpoche, Prof. Namkhai Norbu Rinpoche, Marcopollo, Karl Marx.

Animal Sign: Rabbit
Year: 1999, 1987, 1975, 1963, 1951, 1939, 1927, 1915, 1903, and 1891
Personality:
A person born in this year is a smooth talker, even-tempered, gentle, sociable and respectful to others. They are intelligent but shy by nature. They are compassionate, sharp minded and friendly with others but they are a bit cunning and can be lazy, egotistical and jealous. They are witty, intelligent and fun loving. Love and concern for them often comes from outside. They are soft hearted and diplomatic having the patience and tactics to sort out problems more quickly than others. They are

affectionate, kind, compassionate, virtuous, placid, quietly, and talented by nature. Easy to befriend, good mannered, kind, polite, peaceful by nature, never speak harsh words and are experts in dealing with others. They love communicating with others and everybody praises their nature. They have few enemies and are willing to listen to advice and follow it. They are usually cheerful, brilliant, intellectual, fond of society and diplomatic. They have warm and charming manners. Honest in love and have everlasting friends; sincere and expert in love affairs. They enjoy happy family life generally. They are sharp, observant and fond of lovely things such as fashion, perfumes, and music.

Suitable Occupations: Business, Accountant, Lawyer, Politician, Dancer.

Favourable partner: Sheep, Pig

Unfavourable partner: Bird, Horse, Mouse, Snake and Ox

Famous people had born in this sign: Late Khyabje Yongdzin Ling Rinpoche , Khyabje Trulshik Rinpoche, Garje Khamtrul Jamyang Dhondup Rinpoche, Prof. Samdhong Lobsang Tenzin (Minister), Chogyam Trungpa Rinpoche, Prof. Jampa Gyaltsen Drakthon (late), Confucius, Queen Victoria, Albert Einstein, Martin Luther.

Animal Sign: Dragon

Year: 2000, 1988, 1976, 1964, 1952, 1940, 1928, 1916, and 1904

Personality:

People born in the Dragon year are kind hearted and well disciplined. Everybody likes and praises their behavior and kind nature. They are frank, tactful, honest and sensitive. They can accomplish success in study and business. They talk loudly and have a good heart. They are well mannered and have a beautiful smile. They are hard working and love to complete their work quickly. They are kind hearted, refined and respectable. Broad, open minded, jolly by nature, egotistic, sensitive, impulsive, never lazy and lethargic, brave but not jealous. Clever, excitable, stubborn on the outside, and soft hearted. They are easygoing, willing to take risks, but tend to be more stubborn than most in their thinking and behaviour. They are full of imagination and possess an indomitable spirit. The dragon is decisive when it comes

35

to dealing with anything. They have the potential for accomplishing great things. They are warm, curious and helpful by nature. They are self-centered when it comes to relationships.

Suitable Occupations: Artist, Religious practitioner, Politics, Singer.

Favourable partner: Mouse, Monkey

Unfavourable partner: Dog, Sheep, Ox, Tiger and Horse

Famous people had born in this sign: H.H. Dudjom Rinpoche, Situ Choe-kyi Jungney, Gyalo Dhondup, Jetsun Pema, Sigmund Freud, Frederick IInd the great.

Animal Sign: Snake
Year: 2001, 1989, 1977, 1965, 1953, 1941, 1929, 1917, 1905, and 1893
Personality:
Those born in the Snake year are very ambitious, full of fighting spirit and possess exceptional abilities. They are

clever, sensitive, egotistical and selfish. They are broad-minded and get angry easily. They have a cruel and aggressive nature but are good looking and will always be able to obtain money whenever they need it. They are well spoken but a bit short-tempered by nature. They are broad minded and tolerant. Lovely and quick witted, intelligent and nervous. Fond of music, dance, painting and travels. Extremely wise and attractive but bit self-centered. They are passionate, determined and rather egotistical. A winner with money. Deep thinking and quiet by nature. They are also adaptable, witty and can think far ahead. They are able to get along with everybody. They are quick thinkers and can act according to the situation. They are possessive and jealous by nature.

Suitable Occupations: Teacher, Writer, Nurse, Social work, Public relations, Psychiatrist and Future teller.

Favourable partner: Bird, Ox

Unfavourable partner: Pig, Monkey, Tiger, Sheep and Rabbit

Famous people had born in this sign: Desi Sangye Gyatso, Dorje Chang Jamyang Khyentse Chokyi Lodro, Jigdal Dagchen Sakya, His Holiness the twelfth Tai Situpa, The late Kalu Rinpoche, Zurkhar Lodoe Gyalpo, Amdo Gedun Choephel, Dr. Yeshi Dhondhen (Former physician to H.H. The 14th Dalai Lama), Mohandas Karamchand Gandhi (Gandhiji), Lord Tennyson,

Abraham Lincoln, Pablo Picasso, Charles Robert Darwin, Elizabeth I of England, Mao Zedong.

Animal Sign: Horse
Year: 2002, 1990, 1978, 1966, 1954, 1942, 1930, 1918, 1906, and 1894
Personality:
People born in the year of horse are brave, hard working, well traveled and frank. By nature, they will always listen to others and love animals and sports. They speak loudly and have a nature of walking fast. They are fond of games, have a changeable mind, get hurt easily, are kind towards others, are hard working, creative, tactful, friendly, they want to do by their own wishes, hardly listen other view, have many friends and friendly with them. They also make friends very easily with others but they never trust or believe in others. They are clever and have a well-built body. They love watching movie, writing letters, making phone calls to their friends. They are open minded, showy in dress, quick in everything, handy with

money, cheerful and stubborn. They are very independent and full of enthusiasm in carrying out their duties. They are straightforward, generous with their money, love elaborate events and are good at socialising. They are easy to get along with and have many friends and acquaintances. They are courageous and not afraid of hardship, they usually do very well in their careers. They are lucky in money matters and hence can afford to live in luxury. They sacrifice their own goals in the interest of others.

Suitable Occupations: Scientist, Poetry writer, Politics.

Favourable partner: Tiger, Dog

Unfavourable partner: Mouse, Rabbit, Bird, Dragon and Monkey

Famous people had born in this sign: H.E. Jamgon Kongtrul Rinpoche, New Yuthog Yonten Gompo, Isaac Newton, Chengiz Khan, Lenin.

Animal Sign: Sheep

Year: 2003, 1991, 1979, 1967, 1955, 1943,1931,

1919, and 1907
Personality:
Those born in the sheep year are less talkative, slow and simple. They are passionate and creative. They are friendly and not self-absorbed. They are charming, pious and honest and usually speak less with others. They are patient, zealous and able to overcome any hardship to achieve their goals. They are tolerant and generous by nature and soft spoken. They are frank, independent, brave and can make quick decisions. They are truthful, quarrelsome and have independent views. They are aggressive but very romantic. Most of these people are ambitious, active, energetic and courageous. Best at the arts; their talents will always bring money. They are elegant, charitable, cool, soft and smooth by nature, well mannered, generous in giving alms to others, honest, affectionate, able to help others with their problems and compassionate. They love children and animals and are experts in household life. Everybody praises their behaviour, love in dealing with others and love to wear nice clothes and ornaments, slow in work, give interest to their body. They are refined, loyal and introverted. They also have extraordinary inner strength. They are diplomatic, attentive, considerate towards others and passionate in everything they do. They are pure hearted, extremely loyal and generous.

Suitable Occupations: Gardener, Artist, Government job
Favourable partner: Rabbit, Pig
Unfavourable partner: Ox, Dog, Dragon, Bird and Snake
Famous people had born in this sign: Rev. Khenrab Norbu, Lobsang Samten (Brother of H.H. the 14th Dalai Lama), Johannes Kepler, Benito Mussolini, Thomas Alva Edison, Christopher Columbus.

Animal Sign: Monkey
Year: 2004, 1992, 1980, 1968, 1956, 1944, 1932, 1920, and 1908
Personality:
People born under this sign are sharp-minded, clever by nature and like to go everywhere. They are kind hearted and like to help others. They love to busy themselves and are prone to gossip. They have a quick, witty tongue, love walking and traveling. They are a frank and friendly

with everyone. They prefer to deal with things of their own choosing. They are hyperactive, and convinced of their own superiority. They are intelligent and experts in dealing with others. They are flexible, talented, self-willed and creative people. They enjoy a certain level of popularity in public gatherings or the clubs they join. They are easy going, very adaptable, quick-witted and possess the ability to read situations very well. They are romantic at heart. They pursue fun and entertainment. They are impatient, restless, not easily contented and lack farsightedness. They usually care only about present gain.

Suitable Occupations: Performing arts, Marketing or sales

Favourable partner: Mouse, Dragon

Unfavourable partner: Tiger, Pig, Snake, Dog and Horse

Famous people had born in this sign: Elder Yuthog Yonten Gonpo, H.H. Drubwang Penor Rinpoche, Takpo Tashi Namgyal, Tsering Dolma (Sister of H.H. the 14th Dalai Lama), Dr. Lobsang Wangyal (Senior personal physician to H.H. the 14th Dalai Lama), Leonardo da Vinci, Charles Dickens, Pope John Paul II.

Animal Sign: Bird
Year: 2005, 1993, 1981, 1969, 1957, 1945, 1933, 1921, 1909, and 1897
Personality:
Those born in the Bird year are fond of dance and song. They possess cleanliness and like to wear new clothes. They have strong sexual inclinations and have lots of friends. They can judge others but others find difficulty in judging them. These people are powerful speakers. They are kindhearted and friendly with others. They are rather decisive as well as straight forward by nature. They have strong sense of attachment and often compels them to have friends or acquaintances always around. They are ambitious and intelligent. They cherish cleanliness and love traveling. Deep thinking and short sighted, ambitious and brave, idealistic, sometimes dislike but never boring, well built and good looking, they hardly pass time without friends. Smile, fond of games, clubs and sports. They act after deep consideration, are jovial, generous, love

liberty, independence and freedom. They love to dress up and like wine. Their loyalty, trust and affection are for their partner. They are arrogant, love gossiping, proud and very confident. They usually have good foresight and are perceptive. They often receive praise and compliments from others. They show enthusiasm in the things they do and will not tolerate sloppiness. Money comes and goes easily. They are generally happy and contented people. They are physically light and agile and have a tendency to befriend others.

Suitable Occupations: Tailor, Secretary, Performing arts, Owner of Restaurant, Army, Advertiser.

Favourable partner: Ox, Snake

Unfavourable partner: Rabbit, Mouse, Horse, Sheep and Pig

Famous people had born in this sign: H.H. Sakya Trizin, Kongtrul Yonten Gyatso, Khenpo Jigme Phuntsok Rinpoche, Robindranath Tagore, Peter Usino.

Animal Sign: Dog

Year: 2006, 1994, 1982, 1970, 1958, 1946, 1934, 1922, 1910, and 1898

Personality:

People born in the Dog year are a bit stingy and like to talk a lot. They tend be ambitious, nervous and aggressive. They will often be in two minds about things. They always do their best in their relationships with people. Yet they are selfish and stubborn. They will give wholehearted love and respect to those they love. They take intense care at work and are affectionate towards others. They are impulsive, kind hearted and honest. They are stable minded, hard working and kind-hearted. They love only the person whom they like the most. They are fond of learning, active minded and possess good mental abilities. These people are stubborn, honest, stable minded, hardworking, friendly, affectionate, clever, soft-spoken and impulsive. They are a bit cunning but loyal and faithful by nature. They are quick-thinkers, observant and agile. They have a great sense of humour. They are temperamental by nature and lose their temper easily which might not last long.

Suitable Occupations: Nurse, Beautician, Business, Teacher, Doctor

Favourable partner: Tiger, Horse

Unfavourable partner: Dragon, Ox, Sheep, Mouse and Monkey

Famous people had born in this sign: Rigzin Gyurme Dorje (Terdak glingpa), H.H. Dilgo Khyentse Rinpoche, Drigyung Kyabgon Rinpoche, Lati Rinpoche, Taktse Rinpoche, Ngari Rinpoche, George W. Bush (43rd President of U.S.A), Mother Teresa, Benjamin Franklin, Sir Winston Churchill.

Animal Sign: Pig

Year: 2007, 1995, 1983, 1971, 1959, 1947, 1935, 1923, 1911, and 1899

Personality:

People born under this sign are affectionate and kind to their loved ones and make close life long friends. They are usually good looking, smart, sensitive, and have all the qualities to attract others. They possess tremendous fortune and great honesty. They make friends easily and are extremely loyal to their friends. These people are fond of song and music. They are cheerful and open minded, generous and intelligent. They take intense care of their friendships. They are jolly by nature and generally love to work. They are cool by nature, peaceful, honest and affection towards relatives and beloved ones. They love to help others, possess cleanliness, love setting and decorating rooms, sympathetic and kind. They trust in others, are good hearted, intelligent, dedicated and courageous. They possess a good memory, are very capable of dealing with facts and possess good concentration. They have many friends, and are economical and practical. They are very social but choosy with who become their friends. They are constantly in friendship, quick witted and blessed with a good family and sound financial position. Most of these people are generous and geniuses. They are usually very self-confident and self-centered. They possess good leadership qualities and will stick to whatever they do from beginning to end. They are full of vigor and determination. They are stubborn, gentle and considerate by nature.

Suitable Occupations: Tourism, Lawyer.

Favourable partner: Rabbit, Sheep

Unfavourable partner: Snake, Bird, Tiger, Ox and Monkey

Famous people had born in this sign: Tenzin Gyatso (H.H. The 14th Dalai Lama), Tarthang Tulku Kungeleg, Ven Yudul Trogyal, Lama Norlha, Lady Dr. Lobsang Dolma Khangkar (late).

"Problems can sometimes arise when someone has the same element for the year and the hour. This creates an overabundance of the energy that can work against the person's best interests. In practice, when this happens a much deeper investigation is made to determine the person's elements for the birth month and day."

—**Richard Webster**

How to Find Your Animal Sign (lo rtags)?

Many older Tibetans know very well their animal sign and their whole family's as well. But few know the year when they were born.

So here I have given the calculation to find your animal sign easily.

Take the current year, let's say this year (2002) then subtract your date of birth (year) and add (+) one year to it.

Let's do an example, if someone was born in 1975 and wants to know their animal sign, they would first take the current year, that is 2002, then subtract (–) their birth year from it and add (+) one year which makes their age.

$$
\begin{array}{r}
2002 \\
-1975 \\
\hline
27 \\
+\ 1 \\
\hline
\mathbf{28} \\
\hline
\end{array}
$$

Always start with the current year (gNam-lo), and use the rapid calculation that of 1, 13, 25, 37, 49, 61, 73, 85, 97 and 109 on the current year sign and go counterclockwise and stop at your age that is your birth animal sign.

For example:
A person born in the year 1975 and who is 28 years old. Put the number 25 in the current year sign (because your age is in between 25-37).

Let's work through the process. Place 1, 13, 25 on Horse (current year sign)
26th on Snake
27th on Dragon
28th on Rabbit
So your animal sign is "RABBIT". Now let's find the element for a person who was born in 1975.
There are two methods according to male and female signs of the current year animal sign (gNam-lo).

If the animal sign of the gNam lo (current year) is MALE- (i.e. Mouse, Tiger, Dragon, Horse, Monkey and Dog):
For example, in the year-2002 (Water Horse year), since the Horse is male we must use the following method to find out one's birth element.
1/10-Self (same element as the current year)
2/3-Mother
4/5-Foe
6/7-Friend
8/9-Child

While finding the element, always use the first digit number. Let's say "28" years. 8 is the first digit number and look at the above table (8), the relation is the child. Find the relation of (gnam lo) the current year. So take the element of gnam lo which are Water and the relationship of 1st digit (8) is child. Therefore the child of Water is Wood. So he /she is Wood Rabbit (1975).

If the current year sign is FEMALE (Ox, Rabbit, Snake, Sheep, Bird and Pig) then use this table.

1/2-Self (same element as the current year)
3/4-Mother
5/6-Foe
7/8-Friend
9/10-Child

Let's take another example, say 1978, age 26 years old in next year or 2003.

Place 1, 13, 25 on Sheep, and 26 on Horse.

Now find the element. The next year animal sign is Female (Water Sheep-2003) and the person is 26 years old then look at the "6" in the table above mal sign is Earth Horse.

I will give another example so that you can do this method easily on your own.

If someone is 30 years old in the next year who was born in 1974.

Let's work through the process Put 1, 13, 25 on Sheep,
26 on Horse,
27 on Snake
28 on Dragon
29 on Rabbit
30 on Tiger.

After finding the element, now we have to find the element. I am confident that you can find the sign easily. But you may face some difficulty in finding the element. It is very important to know the current year animal sign first, then the next year, 2003 i.e.; Water Sheep, Sheep belongs to the female group. Looking at the above table we find that "0" is a child. Water (gNam lo) child Wood or the child of Water is Wood. So, he or she is a Wood Tiger.

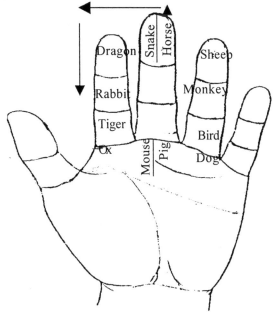

Figure 2 A: To find one's sign

According to the Tibetan Elemental Astrology, one's age refers to the number of calendar years during which one has been alive. The beginning of the year according to the 'byung rtsis system of astrology is consider as the Tiger month (11th Tibetan lunar month) or winter solstice. The difference between Tibetan Astrology and Western Astrology with respect to counting of the Age comes from the way of calculation. In the Tibetan system of Astrology, a person becomes two years just after the

New year, no matter whether twenty four months has past or not. For example, if someone is born in the 9th month (Tibetan Lunar month) of a particular year, the person becomes one year old and then immediately becomes two years old from the 11th month of the following year of the Tibetan Calendar. In this case the person has been alive only two months in the previous year and has started the New Calendar. Therefore the person's age becomes two already. Because the person has gone under the part of two calendar years

Suppose one knows one's animal sign and does not know one's age:

Start with the person's birth animal sign and count clockwise to the current year animal sign (Water- Horse-2002).

This calculation is used only for those who are not certain of their exact age. Always use rapid calculation, that of 1, 13, 25, 37, 49, 61, 73, 85, 97 and 109 to save you time. One cannot calculate their age by knowing only their animal sign. One must know their birth element too.

For example, a woman born in 1975 whose birth sign is **'Wood Rabbit'** and who knows she is under thirty but uncertain of her exact age.

To calculate her exact age first place 1, 13, 25 on her

birth sign (Rabbit), 26 on Dragon, 27 on Snake, 28 on Horse (current year sign), then check the element of 28 years. Since horse is a male, use this method, 1/10-self, 2/3-mother, 4/5-foe, 6/7-friend, 8/9-child. Now look at the above table of '8' (1st digit) and we got child relationship. Therefore, the child of Water is Wood. So, we got Wood Rabbit for 28 years. Therefore he/she is 28 years old and animal sign is Wood Rabbit.

OR

For example, put 1 on your birth sign (i.e. Rabbit)
13 on Rabbit
14 on Dragon
15 on Snake
16 on Horse
17 on Sheep
18 on Monkey
19 on Bird
20 on Dog
21 on Pig
22 on Mouse
23 on Ox
24 on Tiger
25 on Rabbit
26 on Dragon
27 on Snake
28 on Horse (Current year sign-2002).

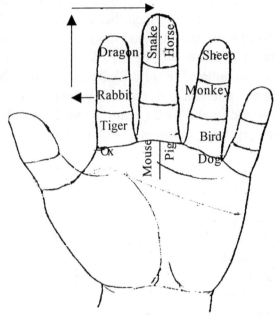

Figure 2 B: To find one's age

If one knows one's age and does not know the animal sign:

First we have to know the animal sign of the current year-2002 which is Water Horse. Start from the Horse and count anticlockwise (counterclockwise) and stop at your age.

Take for example a person who is 22 years old. Let's find his or her animal sign.

Place 1 on Horse (current year animal sign), 13 on Horse, 13 on Horse, 14 on Snake, 15 on Dragon, 16 on Rabbit, 17 on Tiger, 18 on Ox, 19 on Mouse, 20 on Pig, 21 on Dog, 22 on Bird.

This person's animal sign is "Bird". Find the birth element by using the same method explained earlier. So we got the relationship of '2' (1st digit) which is mother relationship. Thus, the mother of Water (current year element) is Metal. Therefore his/her animal sign is Metal Bird.

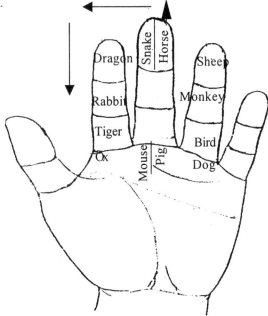

Figure 2 C: To find one's sign

The Sixty-Year Cycle and its Interpretation

The system of the sixty-year cycle is known as Rabjung in Tibetan. It was introduced in the 10th century in Tibet. This system is mainly used to count the years.

The sixty-year cycle is formed under the combination of five elements and 12 animal signs. Each element rules two years in succession and then switch to the next following element, whereas each of the animal sign will rule for one year at a time. For example, if the year 2002 is Water-Horse year, then the year 2003 will be Water-Sheep year.

The first Rabjung was started in the year 1027, associating with the Fire-Rabbit year.

ཤིང་བྱི

Wood Mouse

People born in this sign are intelligent, skilful in craft arts. They are fond of lying and deceive others through their skilful ways. They have moderate wealth and life-styles. However they will be likely to face many ailments due to Naga spirits. Their average lifespan will be seventy-five years. They may have three or five children, and be confronted by seven obstacles.

ཤིང་གླང

Wood Ox

People born in this sign are deep sleepers, stingy, speak less, are violent by nature, and extremely jealous. But they are gifted with intelligence, are long tempered and have big physique. Their average lifespan will be sixty years. Six obstacles will confront them. A person under this group is likely to face obstacles from landlord spirit or wood spirit (shing-gi sadak).

མེ་སྟག

Fire Tiger

People born in this sign are violent, ferocious, physically strong, proud, egoist, possess round eyes, lack faith and are short-tempered. But they are kind hearted, straight forward and speak honestly. They will be harmful to friends who do not help them. They will always be susceptible to internal chronic ailments and generally face phlegm humoural disorders and diseases caused by Naga spirits. They are likely to have two spouses and four children. Their average life span will be seventy-nine years and five obstacles will confront them. A person under this group is born in the educated class. These people may suffer injuries due to a knife or weapons, or get leprosy.

ཨེ་ཡོས

Fire Rabbit

People born in this sign are cowardly, speak less, and and have a divided mind. They will not speak the truth and will act deceitfully, scrutinising the faults of others and telling their own virtues. They will take great pleasure in the company of the opposite sex. They become knowledgeable and an expert without relying on experts or scholars. They will have an average life span of seventy-five years and come across seven obstacles. They will enjoy richness of food, wealth and material resources. They will be afflicted by Landlord spirit and king spirit. They will be most susceptible to serum ailments, cold disorders and severe heart and wind problems.

ས་འབྲུག

Earth Dragon

People born in this sign do not speak the truth and have great speech problems. They will be extremely lazy, short tempered, sleep less, are proud, use harsh words, but love others. They are intelligent, fond of travelling, hard working, health conscious but lack self-confidence, will praise one and defame others. They are fond of alcohol and will commit adultery. They have an average lifespan of fifty-five years and will come across six obstacles. They are likely to have five or seven children. A person under this group is of the educated class. They are deceitful but broad-minded. They will enjoy richness of food, wealth and material resources.

ས་སྦྲུལ

Earth Snake

People born in this sign are broad minded and agile. They will enjoy richness of food, wealth and material resources. There is a high risk of meeting thieves and danger from enemies. Their prosperity will decline and property will be lost. If the person under this category is a male, then may die abroad. Landlord spirit residing on water and trees will cause afflictions. They are lazy, proud, angry, have dark-complexion, black hearted, passionate and jealous. They will take pleasure in the company of evil friends. Their average lifespan will be seventy-nine years and will come across four obstacles. They are likely to have six children. They may commit suicide and get injured by a knife or weapons. These people may suffer from cancerous growths and inflammation of muscle tissue.

ষ্ণ্যাম্'ৰ্চ

Metal Horse

People born in this sign are extremely lazy, short tempered, kind hearted, fond of entertainment, hard working, crave for food and wealth. They show strong love towards relatives. They look for faults in others while neglecting their own faults. They will have an average life span of fifty-seven years and will come across nine obstacles. They will have four children and will face problems in raising children. They may experience much loss of wealth. They are likely to get afflictions from the Landlord spirit and are susceptible to cold disorders and wind ailments.

ལུག་ལྱག

Metal Sheep

People born in this sign are long tempered, bulky with sluggish sense faculties, strong sexual drive, and have poor recollection. They are also susceptible to eye diseases. Their average lifespan will be eighty-one years and they will be come across four obstacles. They are likely to have few children and will be afflicted by Naga spirit and Mount Dwelling spirit (bstan). A person under this group may experience harm often from enemies and disputes.

ཆུ་སྤྲེལ

Water Monkey

People born in this sign are kind hearted, have a divided mind, fond of games, talkative, jealous. They will have an average lifespan of fifty-seven years and will come across seven obstacles. They may become owners of five towns or cities. They may have three children. A person under this group are wealthy and intelligent but may fall victim to blood feuds (dme 'grib).

ཆུ་བྱ།

Water Bird

People born in this sign are health conscious, have good hearing, distracted mind and poor memory retention. They are humble, have strong love towards one's company, have strong sexual drive and are short tempered. They enjoy travelling or walking and come across circle of friends. Their average lifespan will be sixty years and will come across nine obstacles. These people will fall under the sway of others. They will be afflicted by Landlord spirit who abides on trees. Their friends and neighbours may become antagonistic. They are likely to have two children. They are susceptible to fever and wind disorders. A person under this group is deceitful and do not keep their words.

Wood Dog

People born in this sign are passionate, short tempered, talkative, have strong sexual drive, highly skilled, sensitive, high level of recollection and excellent physical appearance. They will have an average life span of seventy-nine years and come across five obstacles. They may become the mayor of a town or city. They are likely to have three children. They will enjoy richness of short-term material resources. However, there is a risk of blood feuds or defilements.

Wood Pig

People born in this sign are fleshy, muscular, wrathful, fierce, egotistical, good physique, beautiful facial appearance, have strong appetite, use harsh words and are thoughtless. They are harmed due to their diet and sexual relations and deceived by friends and lovers. They will have an average lifespan of sixty-four years and will come across five obstacles. The prospect of the family line coming to an end will be less intense by wealth.

ཨེ་བྱི

Fire Mouse

People born in this sign are witty, short tempered, intelligent, talkative, and fast walker. They have many thoughts, many recollections and great craving for wealth and food. They are skilled at exposing the faults of others and they strive to steal and kill. Their average lifespan will be sixty-eight years and they will come across five obstacles. They are susceptible to stomach ailments, diarrhea, and fever and heart disorders.

ཨེ་གླང

Fire Ox

People born in this sign are well built, a bit lethargic, have a faint memory, weak sight, fond of strong drinks, confident, long tempered, and fond of over-sleeping. With an average life span of seventy-one years, they will be confronted by eight obstacles and subjected to afflictions induced by king spirits who frequent temples. They are likely to have one son and two daughters. They will enjoy richness of grain, food, wealth and servants. A person under this group is likely to face eye problems and have slight harm from enemies and evil spirits.

ས་སྟག

Earth Tiger

People born in this sign are fleshy, full of anger, and will take delight in killing. They have great craving for food, are skilled in lying, writings and in delivering speech. There will incur few afflictions due to enemies and evil spirits. They have an average lifespan of seventy-two years and will come across seven obstacles. They are also likely to have two children. A person under this group may be subject to afflictions induced by landlord spirit who abides farm and Naga and Mountain dwelling spirits from a rocky mountain. They are susceptible to tumours and dropsy.

ས་ཡོས

Earth Rabbit

People born in this sign are extremely talkative, knowledgeable and intelligent, but have poor wealth status. They will master grammar and various treatises. Their average lifespan will be fifty years, and six obstacles will confront them. They are likely to have one child. They will commit adultery, enjoy playing games and bring many disasters upon their relatives. They may not enjoy richness of food, wealth and material resources. A person under this group may be subject to afflictions induced by King spirit and Naga spirit. Their grand parents may die from leprosy and they are susceptible to chronic pulmonary disease.

ཕུག་ས་འབྲུག

Metal Dragon

People born in this sign are bulky, egotistical, have stable intelligence, and are strong with great pride. Such people are skilled in speech, and they strive to commit negative deeds, and postpone virtuous actions. They will incur great losses of wealth. They enjoy eating. They do not speak truth, but are fond of disclosing the faults of others. With an average lifespan of Eighty-years, they will be confronted by three obstacles and are likely to have either one or five children. They may be afflicted by king spirits who cause madness. Despite their gentle speech, they are evil within their heart. A person under this group are wealthy, but susceptible to go crazy and mad.

ཤུགས་སྦུལ

Metal Snake

People born in this sign are brilliant and skilled in the craft arts. They take delight in examining the faults of others. They may be theft, and come across enemies and are subjected to many afflictions as they associate with evil friends. Their wealth status is disturbed. They have an average lifespan of seventy-eight years and will come across six obstacles. Their share of food and wealth will be greater in later life than in early life. They will stay with their parents for only a short time and after they have befriended others. Their parents may die due to leprosy or contagious fever. They are likely to have three children. A person under this group are likely to get sudden disease, inflammation of throat, inflammation of muscle tissue and madness.

ཆུ་རྟ

Water Horse

People born in this sign are obedient, extremely intelligent, kind hearted, hard working, fond of racing, wrestling, and fond of barley wine (chang). They do not disclose the faith of others, and they are skilled in craft arts. They will have an abundance of food, wealth and material resources. They are likely to have three or four children and they will be subject to heart and wind disorders and afflictions caused by Landlord spirit. A person under this group is powerful, and do not go under the sway of others. They are wise in digging other's fault and their future goes up and down.

ཆུ་ལུག

Water Sheep

People born in this sign are dull intellect, fond of travelling, skilled in craft arts, have strong sexual drive, weak physical strength. They are passionate and come across five obstacles and are likely to have few children. They enjoy richness of food, wealth and material resources. Their average lifespan will be seventy-three years, and they will come across the danger of thieves and enemies. However, their prosperity will gradually decline and their horses and cattle dispersed. If the concerned person is male he will die abroad. Plaque causing spirit and landlord spirit will harm them and they are susceptible to phlegm humoral disorders.

ཤིང་སྤྲེལ

Wood Monkey

People born in this sign are fleshy, skilled in lying and fond of entertainment. They will come across five obstacles, and are delight in associating with the company of evil friends. They have an average lifespan of seventy-eight years. They have little sleep, many foes and are deceitful. A person under this group will hold two houses and come across many afflictions and disputations. Fluctuation of food is great on them. Mountain Dwelling spirit, landlord spirit and king spirit from river and mountain cliff will harm them. They are likely to have 1 or 5 children.

ཤིང་བྱ

Wood Bird

People born in this sign are kind hearted, have strong sexual drive, short tempered, strong faith to one's life partner, fond of meat and hard drinks like barley wine (chang). They have an average lifespan of sixty years. They are likely to have one or three children. They will meet disputations and quarrel with their near friends and relatives. A person under this group possesses bluish physical complexion and are susceptible to chronic internal disorders.

Fire Dog

People born in this sign are kind hearted, possess long temperament, are talkative, intelligent, have strong sexual drive, skilled in craft arts, passionate and are fond of eating meat. Such people are loved by their higher beings but hatred by people who are below their status. They are likely to come across fevers and bile diseases, and afflictions due to Mountain Dwelling spirits (bstan) and Landlord spirit. They have an average lifespan of sixty-eight years, and will come across seven obstacles. They are likely to have three children.

Fire Pig

People born in this sign have weak body that give way

to many ailments. People of this category may be aggressive, sleepy, unfaithful, and fool and get many dreams. Fever and bile disorders will predominate, but there will also be afflictions due to the mountain dwelling spirit and Landlord spirit. Superiors will grow hostile and their house will be burnt down. They have an average life span of sixty-eight years will come across seven obstacles. They are likely to have three children.

ས་བྱི

Earth Mouse

People born in this sign are wealthy, short in stature, gentle in speech, have light sleep, and take delight in killing. They are lazy and endowed with severe faults. They are susceptible to stomach ailments and may face danger of weapons and knife which take their life. They are selfishly intent upon achieving their own advantage. Their average lifespan will be sixty-eight year and they will come across seven obstacles. They are likely to have one child.

ས་གླང་

Earth Ox

People born in this sign are dull, strong physique, barbarous, persistent and endowed with excessive pride. They will have scanty food, wealth and material resources. They will be afflicted by Landlord spirit. Their mind will be violent, quarrelsome and fierce. They have an average lifespan of fifty years and are likely to have one child. They will come across seven obstacles and slander will arise.

ལྕགས་སྟག

Metal Tiger

People born in this sign are wrathful, fierce and fond of travelling and killing. They have fair complexion, good physique, and a great craving for meat and wine. They speak harshly, and may be afflicted by Mount dwelling spirits and King spirit. They have an average lifespan of sixty years and will come across five obstacles. They are likely to have two or four children. Their share of food, wealth and material resources will be unstable.

ཡོས་
Metal Rabbit

People born in this sign are broad minded, lazy, faithful, hard working, intelligent, kind hearted and knowledgeable. They display loving kindness and generosity to others. There will be afflictions due to blood feuds and Landlord spirit. They have an average lifespan of sixty-one years, and will come across five obstacles. They are likely to have five children. They have an adequate share of food, wealth and material resources. They are susceptible to painful diseases and are likely to face the danger of losing their life under knife and weapons.

ཆུ་འབྲུག
Water Dragon

People born in this sign are egotistical and are fond of using harsh words. They may also display strong pride and have many foolish relatives. They have mole on their bodies and they continuously change their residence. They enjoy archery and other sports. Their family line may come to an end. They have an average lifespan of sixty-two years and will come across six obstacles. They are likely to have one or five children. There is fluctuation in their food and wealth status.

ཆུ་སྦྲུལ

Water Snake

People born in this sign have burning anger in their hearts, are skilled in art of crafts and are egotistical. In friendships they value material resources above people, and they are prepared to indulge in slander. They have an average lifespan of sixty-eight years. They will also be subject to afflictions due to King spirit and Landlord spirit. There is risk of catching cold and wind diseases, and they are likely to have one or five children.

ཤིང་རྟ

Wood Horse

People born in this sign are most deceitful and are difficult to cope and associate. They are endowed with an angry temperament and dull intellect. Their faith and motivation are poor. They have considerable strength and ascetic qualities, are delight in the company of their friends, talkative, shy, fast walker, and are fond of competition like wrestling and other games. They are susceptible to wind and phlegm disorders and meets afflictions caused by King spirit and the Landlord spirit. They have an average lifespan of sixty years and are likely to have one child.

Wood Sheep

People born in this sign are bulky, reliable, less words, craving for wealth, long temperament and kind hearted. They hardly harm others and possess clear sense-faculties. They will have an average lifespan of sixty years and are likely to have two children. They will come across three obstacles. They are foolish and enjoy overeating.

Fire Monkey

People born in this sign have an average lifespan of sixty-seven years, and are susceptible to wind and bile disorders. They take delight in ornaments and clothes, and will come across five obstacles. They may become the headmen of villages, can enjoy abundance of food, wealth and material resources. They are likely to have five children. They use harsh words in speech, are physically strong, have strong pride, fond of digging faults of others, and are talkative, highly intelligent, kind hearted and hard working. A person under this group is egotistical and passionate.

 མེ་བྱ

Fire Bird

People born in this sign are egotistical and passionate. They can assume contrived facial expressions of wrath and make efforts to excel in theft and killing. They have poor recollection and strong desires. Their average lifespan will be sixty-five years and will come across six obstacles. A person under this group is skilled in art of crafts, jealousy, proud, have strong sexual drive, divided mind, and may use harsh words. But they are kind from deep heart, religious, fond of meat and wine and other hard drinks. They are fond of dog and cat very much. There is risk of facing danger from weapons and knife.

ས་ཁྱི

Earth Dog

People born in this sign are short tempered, wrathful, whimsical, talkative and intensely passionate. They will take delight in cursing others and make efforts in sporting contests. They are susceptible to wind and bile disorders. They will dream of befriending the dead and experiencing unhappiness. They will come to possess scant material resources. They are likely to have three or four children. Their average lifespan will be seventy years and confronted by seven obstacles. They are very much fond of sleep and meat.

ས་ཕག

Earth Pig

People born in this sign are violent with speech and fond of fighting. They will bring little benefit to their relatives and acquaintances. They will be afflicted by male spirit (pho 'dre) and Landlord spirit. Their average lifespan will be seventy-seven years and they come across six obstacles. People of this group will have two children, and are rich in food, wealth and material resources. They are health conscious, have little knowledge and will come across much harm from enemy.

ཕྱག་བྱེ

Metal Mouse

People born in this sign are bulky, have light sleep, majestic, intelligent and crave for wealth. They enjoy playing. Their elegance and beauty enable them to stand out from the crowd. They participate in all activities and are faithful. They enjoy fighting and incur great losses of wealth. They play down their own ambitions and gain respect from others. Their average lifespan will be fifty-seven years and will come across six obstacles. They are likely to five children. Their share of wealth and grain will be secure. They will not go under the power of king or boss and gain respect by all. They have few obstacle and enemies. Their ability to harm or benefit others is not potential.

ལྕགས་གླང

Metal Ox

People born in this sign are agile, broad minded, long tempered, and learned in diverse arts of crafts. They face fewer afflictions due to ill health or enemies. People of this kind are prone to sleep and are lazy. They are capable of pleasing friends and kings. Their average lifespan will be fifty-five years and will meet seven obstacles. They are likely to have two children. They are fierce, extremely stubborn and fond of wine and hard drinks. Landlord spirit abiding on water will harm them.

ཆུ་སྟག

Water Tiger

People born in this sign are majestic, possess strong physique and are likely to get divorce from one's partner. They are intelligent, proud, sensitive, and joyful. They have a divided mind. They are creative and extremely fond of games like dice, fond of women and are wealthy. They may speak nobly but hold bad intentions within their hearts. Their average lifespan will be seventy-one years and will come across seven obstacles. They will have one child and there is fluctuation in their food and wealth status.

ཆུ་ཡོས

Water Rabbit

People born in this sign do not place their trust in others. They are fond of business and over sleeping. They will be afflicted by king spirits who abides on charnel grounds and temples. They will dream of falling into a great abyss. Their average lifespan will be seventy-two years and likely to have brave children. People under this group are kind hearted, stingy, double faced, have strong sexual drive and poor memory retention.

ཤིང་འབྲུག

Wood Dragon

People born in this sign are skilled in arts, smooth in speech and easy to associate. They are susceptible to bile diseases, and subject to varying inclinations-sometimes, wishing to travel and sometime wishing to stay at home. Their average lifespan will be sixty-six years and will meet seven obstacles. They are likely to have few children. They will be afflicted by Landlord spirit who abodes on small springs. They enjoy richness of food and wealth. People of this group are loving and kindness, health conscious, and have good hearing sense faculty. They delay in their marriage. Other people envy them greatly.

Wood Snake

People born in this sign are humble, angry, proud, broad minded, stingy and egotistical. They are gifted with tall in stature, and are loved by superiors and hated by inferiors. They are susceptible to few diseases and they will have sons. They will pursue their own interests above others, and will be endowed with an abundance of food, wealth and material resources. Their average lifespan will be seventy-seven years and will meet four obstacles. People under this group are selfish and are fond of associating with evil friends.

ཨེ་ད

Fire Horse

People born in this sign are wrathful and fierce, stubborn and fond of fighting. Their share of wealth will diminish in the long-term. People of this group are intelligent, angry and possess powerful speech. They are fond of fighting and hurting others. They are likely to face fluctuations in their financial status and are fond of dogs and horses. They are susceptible to pulmonary ailments and fevers, as well as afflictions caused by the king spirit. They will meet seven obstacles and will have two children. They have an average lifespan of seventy-eight years.

ཨེ་ལུག

Fire Sheep

People born in this sign are bulky, good personality, hardworking and long lasting in their friendship. They will achieve whatever purpose they have in their mind. Their voices are pleasant, as are their minds. They have a great craving for wealth and will come across seven obstacles. They have an average lifespan of seventy-seven years, and have many children and grandchildren. However, there will be afflictions due to enemies, demons and Landlord spirit. They are likely to face the danger of getting chronic kidney ailments.

ས་སྤྲེལ

Earth Monkey

People born in this sign are easy to associate and cope with. They will have average lifespan of seventy-eight years and come across nine obstacles. They will have three children. Endowed with wealth and cattle. People under this group are having pleasant personality, skilful in delivering talk, kind hearted, divided mind, fond of entertainment, have less pride, gain respect from others and success in every actions they undertake.

ས་བྱ

Earth Bird

People born in this sign are intelligent, short tempered, have strong sexual drive, tough from heart, humble, jealousy, stingy, fond of clothes and ornaments, health conscious, win praise from others, witty, and involve in many actions. Landlord spirit will afflict them. Their vision and sense-faculties will be defective, and they are susceptible to bile diseases. Their average lifespan will be seventy years and will come across seven obstacles. They are likely to have six children.

Metal Dog

People born in this sign are kind hearted, possess pleasant behaviour, have less talk, skilled in arts and crafts, fond of sleep and meat, have strong craving for wealth, have strong sexual drive, jealousy, short tempered, and are loved by the superior beings and hated by people below their status. They will be shy and modest and live in fear of thieves. Their average lifespan will be seventy-seven and will come across seven obstacles. They will have three or four children.

Metal Pig

People born in this sign are proud, egotistical, does not keep their words and fond of sleep. They possess great appetite, endowed with great power and wealth. They will have two or four children and come across seven obstacles. Their average lifespan will be seventy years. They will gain respect from others and material as well.

Water Mouse

People born in this sign are extremely elegant, calm, jealousy, have strong sexual drive and deceitful. They have great craving for food and wealth and harmful to one's neighbour. Their average lifespan will be seventy-two years. They will come across seven obstacles and will have two or five children. They may face great decline of wealth and food. Afflictions will come due to Landlord spirit and plague causing spirit (gnyen) who abides on woods at the east.

ཆུ་གླང

Water Ox

People born in this sign are extremely foolish, fond of oversleeping, and lazy. They have great physique, unpleasant voice, use harsh words, and are selfish. They are broad-minded, and are fond of wine and hard drinks. They will have average lifespan of seventy years and come across seven obstacles. Even though they may speak gently to others, ultimately they will engage in many deceitful actions. They will be afflicted by Landlord spirit from the cremation and charnel ground.

ཤིང་སྟག

Wood Tiger

People born in this sign are wrathful, fierce, energetic, and are fond of fighting. Their average lifespan will be sixty-six years. They are susceptible to tumours, dropsy, inflammation of muscle tissue and throat. They will have three children and come across five obstacles. They will consider other people as foolish, and they are likely to face death under knife or weapons. Such people are clever, jealousy, angry, powerful and selfish.

ཤིང་ཡོས

Wood Rabbit

People born in this sign are crafty, have strong sexual drive, fond of games, songs, dances, egotistical, divided mind and friendly with others. Their average lifespan will be sixty-seven years. They will have many fears due to ill health and enemies. They will have children in early and later life and, will come across six obstacles. A person under this group may commit adultery.

Fire Dragon

People born in this sign are bulky, short tempered, truthful, intelligent, skilful in the art of crafts, health conscious, praise oneself, fine tongue, and are wealthy. If they are householders they will marry a widowed person. They will have good appetites. Their average lifespan will be seventy-one years and come across seven obstacles. They will have two children. They are susceptible to combined wind and bile disorders. They will acquire an abundance of food, wealth and material resources. They are likely to come across the risk of thieves and enemies.

ཨེ་སྦྲུལ

Fire Snake

People born in this sign are lazy, subject to few diseases, and endowed with many friendships. They will marry five or 7 spouses and will become rich. Their average lifespan will be seventy-one years and will meet seven obstacles. They are likely to have two children. They will face problems from thief and enemies. People under this group are bulky, skilled in art of craft, expert on literature and treatise, tough from inside and have strong sexual drive. They are susceptible to wind bile diseases and they may die under the knife or weapon.

ས་རྟ

Earth Horse

People born in this sign are brave, kind hearted, short tempered, altruistic, gain respect, are fond of travelling, faithful, walk fast, have clear voice, and are intelligent.

They laugh loudly. Their average lifespan will be sixty-five years and will have two children. They will face seven obstacles. A person under this group is likely to face the harm and danger from enemies or diseases.

Earth Sheep

People born in this sign are prone to many diseases and go in fear of enemies. Their average life span will be sixty years and face four obstacles. If they are male subjects they will be drawn to their daughters and female to their sons. People under this group are possessing gentle personality. Outsider's will loved them but hatred by their family members. They are dull, selfish and are egotistical.

ལུགས་སྤྲེལ

Metal Monkey

People born in this sign are kind hearted, selfish, divided mind and loved by all who set eyes upon them. They are extremely beautiful and attractive, and will have an abundance of wealth and material resources. They are energetic. Their average lifespan will be seventy years and face seven obstacles. They are likely to have one or five children. They will go under fear of war and enemies. Happiness will come when they become old. A person under this group may cause blood feuds.

ཕུགས་བུ

Metal Bird

People born in this sign are glorious and masterful. They endowed with much wealth, grain and an abundance of food and drink. They will become leaders of mankind. There will be afflictions due to demons associated with blood feuds and leprosy-causing demons. People under this group are short tempered, kind hearted, have strong sexual drive, powerful, humble, have light sleep, gentle in speech, trustworthy, expert in delivering speech, love one's teachers and relatives, and fond of meat and hard drinks like wine etc. Their average lifespan will be seventy years and face seven obstacles. They are likely to have four children. They are susceptible to wind diseases and fevers.

ཆུ་ཁྱི

Water Dog

People under this group are sluggish, have strong attachment, are stingy and have strong sexual drive. They are fond of fighting, quarrelling and face danger from enemy and weapons. Their average lifespan will be seventy-three years and will be afflicted by evil spirits, demons, Landlord spirit, and king spirit. They are likely to have few children and little wealth. Their bodies have many ugly marks and are generally susceptible to ill health and injuries.

ཆུ་ཕག

Water Pig

People born in this sign are proud, jealousy and have heavy sleep. They are fond of using bad words and gain less respect from others. They are likely to have four children. They are gifted with knowledge; possess stable intelligence but bit egotistical. They will own cows, food, property and grain. There will be a risk of suicide or fatal falls. Their average life span will be sixty years and will come five obstacles.

Changeable Animal Sign (Lok men):

According to the Elemental Astrology texts:

"De yang log men brtsi tshul ni
kyes pa rang rang dbang thang gi
Bu yi sTag nas thur du sBubs
rang rang lo grangs gang yin bgrang
De yis log men 'khrul med rnyed
Bud med dbang thang ma yi sprel
Gyen du lo grangs bar bken pas
Gang babs lo de log men yin"

Each person has a birth sign and a changeable sign. The birth sign remains constant, but the changeable sign (derived sign) will change from year to the next according to the changes of the year-cycle. There are two methods for finding your changeable sign (lok men).

If the concerned person is male, one should determine whichever the 5 elements has a child relationship with the power element. And count forwards from the Tiger or begin from Tiger and count age downwards.

If the concerned person is female, one should determine whichever of the five elements forms a mother relationship with the power element, and count backwards from the Monkey.

Example:

A 48 years old man has the animal sign Wood Sheep. Since this person is a male, count downwards from the

Tiger (*Tiger, Rabbit, Dragon, Snake, Horse, Sheep, Monkey, Bird, Dog, Pig, Mouse and Ox*) to the number of his age (i.e. 48 years), and we find **Ox**. After that we have to know his birth element which is Wood to find the element. The child of Wood is Fire-1, The child of Fire is Earth-13, The child of Earth is Metal-25, The child of Metal is Water-37, Water-38, Wood-39, Wood-40, Fire-41, Fire-42, Earth-43, Earth-44, Metal-45, Metal-46, Water-47, **Water-48**

Therefore his changeable animal sign (log men) of this year is **Water Ox**.

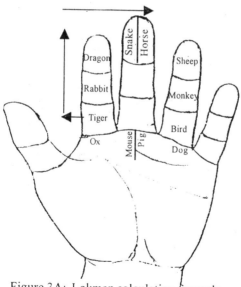

Figure 3A: Lokmen calculation for male

95

Table no. 6
Changeable Animal sign (log men)

Sign	Tiger	Rabbit	Dragon	Snake	Horse	Sheep	Mon-key	Bird	Dog	Pig	Mouse	Ox
Ages	1	2	3	4	5	6	7	8	9	10	11	12
	13	14	15	16	17	18	19	20	21	22	23	24
	25	26	27	28	29	30	31	32	33	34	35	36
	37	38	39	40	41	42	43	44	45	46	47	48
	49	50	51	52	53	54	55	56	57	58	59	60
	61	62	63	64	65	66	67	68	69	70	71	72
	73	74	75	76	77	78	79	80	81	82	83	84
	85	86	87	88	89	90	91	92	93	94	95	96
	97	98	99	100	1	2	3	4	5	6	7	8

If the concerned person is a female:

Always start from Monkey (Monkey, Sheep, Horse, Snake, Dragon, Rabbit, Tiger, Ox, Mouse, Pig, Dog and Bird) and work anti clockwise.

For instance: A lady who is 48 years old (Female) has the sign Wood Sheep. Use the mother elemental relationship from the birth element. The birth element is most important in this system. It is quite different from the male formula. After stopping at 37 years, you must jump to the next element i.e. Wood. In the Male formula, the element of 38 years is Fire (same as 37 years) whereas in the female formula, Wood is for 38.

The mother of Wood is Water-1

The mother of Water is Metal-13

The mother of Metal is Earth-25

The mother of Earth is Fire-37

The mother of Fire is Wood-38

Wood-39

Water-40

Water-41

Metal-42

Metal-43

Earth-44

Earth-45

Fire-46

Fire-47

Wood-48

After that let's find the animal sign, start from Monkey, and count anti clockwise up to your age that is Bird. Therefore her changeable sign of this year is **Wood Bird**.

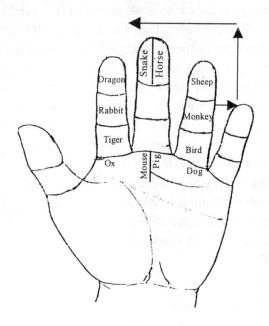

Figure 3B: Lokmen calculation for female

Table no. 7

Changeable Animal sign (log men)

Sign / Ages	Monkey	Sheep	Horse	Snake	Dragon	Rabbit	Tiger	Ox	Mouse	Pig	Dog	Bird
	1	2	3	4	5	6	7	8	9	10	11	12
	13	14	15	16	17	18	19	20	21	22	23	24
	25	26	27	28	29	30	31	32	33	34	35	36
	37	38	39	40	41	42	43	44	45	46	47	48
	49	50	51	52	53	54	55	56	57	58	59	60
	61	62	63	64	65	66	67	68	69	70	71	72
	73	74	75	76	77	78	79	80	81	82	83	84
	85	86	87	88	89	90	91	92	93	94	95	96
	97	98	99	100	1	2	3	4	5	6	7	8

Table no. 8
Recognition of changeable sign element (Log men dbang khams)

Male Birth Element →	Wood	Fire	Earth	Metal	Water	Ages of Female person ↓
1/2	Fire	Earth	Metal	Water	Wood	8/9
3/4	Earth	Metal	Water	Wood	Fire	6/7
5/6	Metal	Water	Wood	Fire	Earth	4/5
7/8	Water	Wood	Fire	Earth	Metal	2/3
9/10	Wood	Fire	Earth	Metal	Water	1/10
↑ Ages of Male person	Fire	Earth	Metal	Water	Wood	← Female Birth Element

"The quantity of each element determines our personalities and degree of success in life. It takes a highly skilled astrologer to successfully balance and interpret the effects of these five elements in our horoscopes."

—Richard Webster

How to Find Your Life Force (srog), Body (lus), Power (dbang thang), Luck (klung rta) and Life Soul (bla)?

Calculation of life force, body, power, luck and life soul plays a vital role in Elemental Astrology. Different people have a different srog (life force), lus (body), dbang thang (wealth) and klung rta (fortune), which will remain constant throughout your lifetime.

The five categories of life are life force, body, power, luck and life soul, which are listed in order of importance.

1) Life force; one's life span: Life force is the most important from the five. It has the unique characteristic of sustaining life. If one can have a long life span, there is an ample opportunity to spend one's life in a more meaningful way. For example, one could practice religion and use this precious life for the service of others, which will bring happiness in this life and as well as next life.

2) Body; one's overall bodily or physical condition: Even if one's life force or sRog in the table shows a long life span, if we lack physical well being we have little chance of enjoying our worldly wealth.

3) Power/wealth; both economic or political power: Though one may possess a stable life force and good health to undertake any peaceful or violent work, power is indispensable for it. Power is the potency that changes the direction of work to the positive side.

4) Luck; overall luck in business or work: Literally means "wind horse". With good life force, sound health and power one is able to do any kind of religious or political activities. Luck plays a vital role in leading a successful life.

5) Life soul: Bla is loosely translated as life soul. It is read as La. It is the fundamental life essence energy which is responsible for the integration of our consciousness with our body. La (Bla) can be lost or taken captive by evil spirits. A person who lost the life soul is characterised by tiredness, pale, frightened, dull, passive, weak physical strength, and lost of physical and facial radiance. In such case, it is important to refer this person to high Lama and tantric practitioners for recalling the lost life soul. Failing to do this results in untimely death.

Calculation of Life Force (srog), Body (lus), Power (dbang thang), Luck (klung rta) and Life Soul (bla).

Life force (srog):

To work out some one's life force element, one considers only the animal sign of the year of birth and not the element. It is the simplest method of finding one's srog (Life force). The life force element of the year sign refers to the elements associated with their respective locations.

In the Elemental Text "'byung rtsis man ngag zla ba'i 'od zer":

"srog ni gnas phyog 'byung ba ste
stag yos srog shing rta sbrul me
bya sprel lcags la byi phag chu
glang lug khyi 'brug bzhi srog sa"

The Topside of the square represents South, the element Fire, and the animal sign Horse and Snake. Therefore the life force of the Horse and the Snake is Fire.

The Lower side represents North and the element Water (Mouse and Pig). The life force of the Mouse and the Pig is Water.

The Left hand side represents East and the element Wood (Tiger and Rabbit). The life force of the Tiger and the

Rabbit is Wood.

The Right side represents West and the element Metal (Bird and Monkey). The life force of the Bird and the Monkey is Metal.

The Four corners correspond to the four midway points of the compass and the element Earth (Ox, Sheep, Dog and Dragon). The life force of the Ox, Sheep, Dog and Dragon is Earth.

For example, let's find the life force element of a person whose animal sign is Monkey. The life force element would be Metal as the Monkey is to be found on the West side of the square, which corresponds, to Metal. You can use the same method for the rest of the animal signs.

Table no. 9
Life force element

Direction	East	South	Four Cardinal	West	North
Elements	Wood	Fire	Earth	Metal	Water
Animal Signs	Tiger, Rabbit	Horse, Snake	Ox, Sheep, Dog, Dragon	Bird, Monkey	Mouse Pig

Body (lus):

Calculating the body (lus) is complicated and has to go with the long procedure. There are two different ways of finding the lus (body) element. You must memorize all the keys first, then use either step.

According to the Elemental Astrology text 'byung rtsis zla bai vod zer".

"De ni lus kyi lde mig ni
stag yos bya sprel kham nas rtsi
glang lug rta byi zin nas rtsi
Khyi 'brug phag sbrul da nas rtsi
lchags chu me sa shing du bgrang"

The key of Tiger, Rabbit, Bird, and Monkey is Kham (Water).

The key of Ox, Sheep, Horse and Mouse is Zin (Wood).

The key of Dog, Dragon, Pig and Snake is Da (Metal).

The key of each element has to be checked against your birth element and then see whether the relationship is of Mother, child, foe, and friend. If the relationship is mother, then the body element is Wood etc., check the following given below.

Mother-Wood
Child-Water
Friend-Fire
Foe-Earth

Same-Metal (if the key element and birth element are same, the body element is Metal).

For example, if the key element is Metal and your birth element is Wood, check the relationship of Metal to Wood, which is a friend relationship. The friend of Metal is Wood. Since it is the friend relationship then the body element (lus) is FIRE. If the relation is Mother, the element is Wood. If the relation is child, the element is Water. If the relation is friend, the element is Fire. If the relation is foe, the element is Earth. If both are same element - the element is Metal.

OR

Another way of finding body element (lus). In the case of persons born in the Tiger, Rabbit, Bird and Monkey, one can calculate from the Water.

It is calculated from the Wood element in the case of persons born in the Ox, Sheep, Horse and Mouse year. In the case of person born in the Dog, Dragon, Pig and Snake year, one can calculated from the Metal element.

Calculation:

Start from your key element (let's say Tiger, the key element of Tiger is Water), put the Metal (key element) on it and stop at your birth element. Place the elements (METAL, WATER, FIRE, EARTH, AND WOOD) on the actual element, i.e. Wood on thumb, Fire on forefinger, Earth on middle finger, Metal on ring finger and Water on little finger.

Take an example, a person born in 1972 whose animal sign is Water Mouse. Since the key element of Mouse is Wood. So, count from the Wood element, put METAL on Wood, WATER on Fire, FIRE on Earth, EARTH on Metal and WOOD on Water (stop here because his/her birth element is Water). So his/her body (lus) is Wood.

Table no. 10
Body element

Wood	Fire	Earth	Metal	Water
Metal Tiger	Fire Tiger	Earth Tiger	Water Tiger	Wood Tiger
Metal Rabbit	Fire Rabbit	Earth Rabbit	Water Rabbit	Wood Rabbit
Earth Dragon	Wood Dragon	Fire Dragon	Metal Dragon	Water Dragon
Earth Snake	Wood Snake	Fire Snake	Metal Snake	Water Snake
Water Horse	Earth Horse	Metal Horse	Wood Horse	Fire Horse
Water Sheep	Earth Sheep	Metal Sheep	Wood Sheep	Fire Sheep
Iron Monkey	Fire Monkey	Earth Monkey	Water Monkey	Wood Monkey
Metal Bird	Fire Bird	Earth Bird	Water Bird	Wood Bird
Earth Dog	Wood Dog	Fire Dog	Metal Dog	Water Dog
Earth Pig	Wood Pig	Fire Pig	Metal Pig	Water Pig
Water Mouse	Earth Mouse	Metal Mouse	Wood Mouse	Fire Mouse
Water Ox	Earth Ox	Metal Ox	Wood Ox	Fire Ox

Power (dbang thang):

The power element is the same as the element that rules the year.

To do this, it is necessary to have at least some idea of the animal cycles as defined by the Tibetan Calendar. The 12 animal sign are always combined with the five elements. Each element rules for two years in succession. Combining the twelve animals and the five elements gives rise to a cycle of 60 years, called 'Logan Dugchu' or sixty year cycle. In this cycle each of the twelve animals appear five times, each time coupled with different elements.

For example, 2002 is a Water Horse year. Therefore a child born this year would be Water Horse and their power element (wangthang) would be the Water.

The power (wangthang) element of a child born in 2003 (Water Sheep), or in 2004 (Wood Monkey year) would be Water and Wood respectively.

Table no. 11
Wangthang (Power)

Wood	Mouse	Dog	Monkey
	Ox	Pig	Bird
	Horse	Dragon	Tiger
	Sheep	Snake	Rabbit
Fire	Tiger	Mouse	Dog
	Rabbit	Ox	Pig
	Monkey	Horse	Dragon
	Bird	Sheep	Snake
Earth	Dragon	Tiger	Mouse
	Snake	Rabbit	Ox
	Monkey	Horse	Dragon
	Pig	Bird	Sheep
Metal	Horse	Dragon	Tiger
	Sheep	Snake	Rabbit
	Mouse	Dog	Monkey
	Ox	Pig	Bird
Water	Monkey	Horse	Dragon
	Bird	Sheep	Snake
	Tiger	Mouse	Dog
	Rabbit	Ox	Pig

Fortune (klungta):

Once again one refers to the twelve animals and their relationship to the elements. If you want to know your luck/fortune elements then one must memorise a few key lines, which are the elements of fortune in the Elemental Astrology text.

"stag rTa khyi gsum klung sprel lchags
Byi 'brug sprel gsum klung stag shing
bya glang sbrul gsum klung phag chu
phag lug yos gsum klung sbrul me"

Tiger, Horse, and Dog- Metal
Mouse, Dragon, and Monkey-Wood
Bird, Ox, and Snake -Water
Pig, Sheep, and Rabbit-Fire
This is the easiest method among all the four (life force, body, power and luck). Start from one animal sign (any of them) and skip the next four animals and take the next sign and again skip four animal signs and take the next sign. Continue this process.

Take an example, the fortune element of a child born in a Tiger, Horse or Dog year would therefore be Metal.

Table no. 12
Fortune Element

Wood	Fire	Metal	Water
Mouse, Dragon, Monkey	Pig, Sheep, Rabbit	Tiger, Horse, Dog	Bird, Ox, Snake

Soul (bla):

The calculation of bla (soul) is very simple. All that needs to be known is the person's life force element. The bla is just the mother of the life force.
"Srog gi ma ni bla ru grags"

Take for example someone born in a Tiger year. Their life force element is Wood, so they will have Water as bla because the mother element of Wood is Water.

Table no. 13
Life soul Element

Wood	Fire	Earth	Metal	Water
Horse, Snake	Ox, Sheep, Dog, Dragon	Bird, Monkey	Mouse, Pig	Tiger, Rabbit

"The Seasonal pulse (dus-rtsa), Healthy pulse (nad-med-rtsa), Sickness pulsa (nad-rtsa), Constitutional pulsa (rgyun-rtsa) and Seven wonderful pulses (ngo-mtsar-rtsa-bdun) are all mainly examined on the basis of Mother-Child and Friend-Foe calculation.
Moreover, the urinalysis and examination of major organs and their related sense organs also involves the calculation of elements. In order to facilitate us in making a correct judgement between seasonal pulse, general pulse and specific pulse etc, we have to use the aid of astrological knowledge."
—Dr. Tsering Thakchoe Drungtso

Calculation of Animal Sign of Year (lo), Month (daba), Day (zhag) and Hour (dus) Combining with the Five Elements:

The calculation of the twelve animal signs and 5 elements has always been done together, to observe the periodic change of year, month, day and hour with a specific name in the Elemental Astrology.

Year (lo): Each year is ruled by one of the five elements and one of the twelve animal signs. The Mouse year stands at the beginning of the cycle since the foremost landlord King "These", was located in the lower North (byang smad) direction, coinciding with the Mouse.

The twelve years cycle (Mouse, Ox, Tiger, Rabbit, Dragon, Snake, Horse, Sheep, Monkey, Bird, Dog, Pig) combined with the five elements (Wood, Fire, Earth, Metal, Water) that give the cycle of sixty years (lo rgan drug chu). Each of the elements is associated with two animal signs. The sixty years begins from Wood Mouse and end at Water Pig. The animal signs keeps on changing every year, which is shown in the table below. For example, if someone is born in the year 2002, the animal sign of that year is Water Horse, so anyone born in 2002 has the animal sign Water Horse.

1912/1972	1913/1973	1914/1974	1915/1975
Water Mouse	Water Ox	Wood Tiger	Wood Rabbit
1916/1976	**1917/1977**	**1918/1978**	**1919/1979**
Fire Dragon	Fire Snake	Earth Horse	Earth Sheep
1920/1980	**1921/1981**	**1922/1982**	**1923/1983**
Metal Monkey	Metal Bird	Water Dog	Water Pig
1924/1984	**1925/1985**	**1926/1986**	**1927/1987**
Wood Mouse	Wood Ox	Fire Tiger	Fire Rabbit
1928/1988	**1929/1989**	**1930/1990**	**1931/1991**
Earth Dragon	Earth Snake	Metal Horse	Metal Sheep
1932/1992	**1933/1993**	**1934/1994**	**1935/1995**
Water Monkey	Water Bird	Wood Dog	Wood Pig
1936/1996	**1937/1997**	**1938/1998**	**1939/1999**
Fire Mouse	Fire Ox	Earth Tiger	Earth Rabbit
1940/2000	**1941/2001**	**1942/2002**	**1943/2003**
Metal Dragon	Metal Snake	Water Horse	Water Sheep
1944/2004	**1945/2005**	**1946/2006**	**1947/2007**
Wood Monkey	Wood Bird	Fire Dog	Fire Pig

Month (dawa):

According to the Elemental Astrological system, the beginning of the year is considered as the 11th Tibetan Lunar month (Tiger month because the Winter solstice occurs in the 1st spring month of the Tiger. It is called lo 'go in Tibetan which means beginning of the year. The twelve animal sign characterises the twelve months, beginning with Tiger, the sign for the eleventh month, and ending in the tenth month (Ox) of the ensuing year.

Tiger represents 11th month (1st Spring)
Rabbit represents 12th month (Mid Spring)
Dragon represents 1st month (Last Spring)
Snake represents 2nd month (1st Summer)
Horse represents 3rd month (Mid Summer)
Sheep represents 4th month (Last Summer)
Monkey represents 5th month (1st Autumn)
Bird represents 6th month (Mid Autumn)
Dog represents 7th month (Last Autumn)
Pig represents 8th month (1st Winter)
Mouse represents 9th month (Mid Winter)
Ox represents 10th month (Last Winter)

Calculation:

It is important to clearly understand the element of the current year first and then use the child elemental relationship from it. Place always the 1st child elemental relationship on the 11th and 12th month. Let's say this year 2002 (Water Horse year). The child of Water is Wood. Therefore 11th and 12th month is Wood. In the 1st and 2nd month, the element would be the child of Wood i.e. Fire etc

Let's find the animal sign and element of the 6th month. You can find the sign very easily by looking at the above table.

Start from the 11th month Tiger, and go clockwise past 12th Rabbit, 1st Dragon etc. until we stop at the 6th month which is Bird month.

Now find the element of the 6th month. First we have to know the element of the current year 2002-Water Horse. Using the aforementioned idea, the child of Water (current year element) is Wood. Place the Wood element on the 11th and 12th month, the child of Wood is Fire which is for 1st and 2nd, 3rd and 4th is Earth, 5th and 6th is Metal. The element of the 6th month is Metal and the sign is Bird (Look at the above table). So the element and sign is Metal Bird for the 6th month.

1st Month **Dragon**	2nd Month **Snake**	3rd Month **Horse**	4th Month **Sheep**
12th Month **Rabbit**			5th Month **Monkey**
11th Month **Tiger**			6th Month **Bird**
10th Month **Ox**	9th Month **Mouse**	8th Month **Pig**	7th Month **Dog**

Table no. 15
Animal sign of month

Day (zhag):

One must know the month (element and animal sign) first while finding the day. It is very important to know that whether the month sign is a male or female otherwise you will find it wrong. After finding the month, Metal Bird, you must then check whether the month sign is male or female.

For the six male months (Mouse, Tiger, Dragon, Horse, Monkey, and Dog), the 1st day is counted from the Tiger sign, 2nd Rabbit, 3rd Dragon, 4th Snake, 5th Horse, 6th Sheep, 7th Monkey, 8th Bird, 9th Dog, 10th Pig, 11th Mouse, 12th Ox, 13th Tiger, 14th Rabbit, full moon coincides with the Dragon day and new moon with the Sheep day.

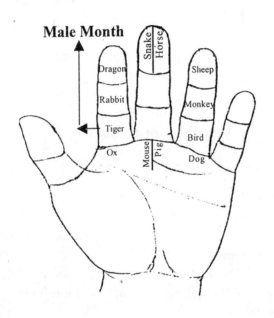

Figure 4 A: For male month

118

Whereas in the case of the six female months (Ox, Rabbit, Snake, Sheep, Bird and Pig), the 1st day always counted from the Monkey, 2nd Bird, 3rd Dog, 4th Pig, 5th Mouse, 6th Ox, 7th Tiger, 8th Rabbit, 9th Dragon, 10th Snake, 11th Horse, 12th Sheep, 13th Monkey, 14th Bird, full moon coincides with the Dog day and new moon with the Ox day.

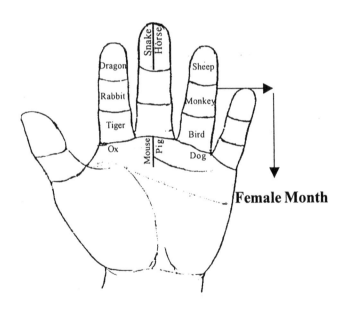

Figure 4 B: For male month

These same animal signs (Tiger/Monkey) therefore reappear as the 1st, 13th and 25th calendar days of the Tibetan lunar month.

Example:
Let's find the animal sign and element of the 14th day since the month (6th) is Metal Bird, which is female.
Place 1st and 13th on Monkey, 14th on Bird. Now find the element, the child of Metal (6th month) is Water. So place 1st/6th day on Water, 2nd/7th on Wood, 3rd/8th on Fire, 4th/9th on Earth. Earth is the element of the 14th day and the animal sign of 14th day is Bird. So the 14th day is Earth Bird.

Hour (dus):

In earlier days in Tibet, there were no watches or clocks, so all the nomads, farmers and layperson would measure the time by putting water in a vase or pot with a hole in the bottom.

The other ancient system of measuring time was by looking at the shadow of the sun. They used the traditional special name of the time based on the animal signs to read it out. The traditional name of the hour is still continuously used among the farmers and nomads in Tibet.

Referencing the information below, let's find the animal sign for the time, 10.00 a.m. which is Snake. Now, we have to find the element of the hour. Use the child relationship from the day element (Earth Bird-14th day). Therefore the child of Earth is Metal- 5 to 6.59 a.m., the child of Metal is Water-7 to 8.59 a.m., the child of Water is Wood-9 to 10.59 a.m. Thus, the element for the time 10.00 a.m. is Wood Snake

1) 5-6.59 a.m. Namlang yos (Rabbit)-Day break,
2) 7-8.59 a.m. Nyishar 'brug (Dragon)-Sun rise,
3) 9-10.59 a.m. Nyi dros sbrul (Snake)-Morning,
4) 11-12.59 p.m. Nyin phyed rta (Horse)-Noon,
5) 1-2.59 p.m. Phyed yol lug (Sheep)- Afternoon,
6) 3-4.59 p.m. Nyi myur sprel (Monkey)-Late afternoon.
7) 5-6.59 p.m. Nyi nub bya (Bird)-Sun set,
8) 7-8.59 p.m. Sa sros khyi (Dog)-Dusk,
9) 9-10.59 p.m. Sros khor phag (Pig)-Forenight,
10) 11-12.59 a.m. Nam phyed byi (Mouse)-Mid night,
11) 1-2.59 a.m. Nam yol glang (Ox)-After mid night,
12) 3-4.59 a.m. Tho rengs stag (Tiger)-Dawn.

Tibetan Elemental Astrology

Table no. 16
Animal sign of hour

7-8.59 a.m. Dragon	9-10.59 a.m. Snake	11-12.59 p.m. Horse	1-2.59 p.m. Sheep
5-6.59 a.m. Rabbit			3-4.59 p.m Monkey
3-4.59 a.m. Tiger			5-6.59 p.m. Bird
1-2.59 a.m. Ox	11-12.59 a.m. Mouse	9-10.59 p.m. Pig	7-8.59 p.m. Dog

Know Your Good and Bad Day:

Each of the twelve animal is associated with three weekdays. Soul day (bla-gza), and life force day (srog gza) are favourable or lucky day. Whereas foe day (gshed-gZa) is bad day or unfavourable day. The soul day and life force day are good for making important decisions, meeting important people, changing house, travelling, moving to other place, spiritual practice, and starting new projects etc. Whereas, during the gshed-gZa, it would be extremely unfavourable and unlucky for you to start or carry out any of the activities mentioned above. In case you are compelled to carry out such activities on unfavourable day, there are specific remedial measure and rituals recommended in the Tibetan Astrological text which will prevent the negative influences from affecting you and your works. The ritual or remedial measure are highly powerful. In the Tibetan saying "Performing ritual or remedial measure is like a child play but the benefit coming from them is like great Mount Meru". However, sometimes unfavourable days may turn into positive (favourable) days for those whose birth took place during an unfavourable day.

Before you start finding your good and bad day, you must know the elements of the weekdays. The Fire element corresponds to Sunday and Tuesday.

The Water element corresponds to Monday and Wednesday.
The Wood element corresponds to Thursday.
The Metal element corresponds to Friday.
The Earth element corresponds to Saturday.

According to the elemental Astrology text:
The life force of Tiger and Rabbit is Wood.
The life force of Horse and Snake is Fire.
The life force of Monkey and Bird is Metal.
The life force of Mouse and Pig is Water
The life force of Ox, Sheep, Dog and Dragon are Earth.
Take for example a person whose sign is Tiger. Since the life force element of the Tiger and Rabbit is Wood, and the Wood element is connected with the weekday Thursday. Therefore, the soul day of a person born under Tiger and Rabbit sign is Thursday.
After finding the soul day, we have to find the life force day and foe day using the friend and foe elemental relationship. Since the life force of Tiger/Rabbit is Wood, use the friend relationship to find the life force day. Thus, the friend of Tiger/Rabbit (Wood) is Earth. Earth is connected with Saturday. So Saturday is his/her life force day. Now find the foe day, which is an enemy relationship. We discover the enemy of Wood (Tiger/Rabbit) is Metal. Friday is related to the Metal element. Thus the foe day

of the Tiger and Rabbit is Friday. You can use the same method for the rest of the animal signs to find out a person's good and bad days. However, one must be very careful while finding the favourable and unfavourable day of the four cardinal signs i.e. Dragon, Sheep, Dog and Ox, the Earth elements. As we all know that, the twelve animal signs are in row, so next to the Dragon, we find the Snake. The life force of the Snake is Fire (Sunday). Therefore, the fire element (Sunday) becomes Dragon's soul day. Likewise, when finding the soul day of Sheep, we discover Monkey as the Monkey is next to the Sheep, so the life force of Monkey is Metal (Friday). Thus, the soul day of the Sheep is Friday. Similarly, when finding the soul day for Dog we discover the sign next to Dog is Pig. So, the life force of Pig is Water. Thus, the soul day of Dog is Monday. The soul day of Ox is Saturday. Since the life force of Ox is Earth. The friend of Earth is Water which is related to the Wednesday. Therefore, the lifeforce day of Ox, Sheep, Dog and Dog are Wednesday. The enemy of Earth is Wood (Thursday). Thus Thursday becomes their foe day or bad day.

Table no. 17
Good and bad day

Animal Sign	Soul day	Life force day	Foe day
Mouse/Pig	Wednesday	Tuesday	Saturday
Ox	Saturday	Wednesday	Thursday
Tiger/Rabbit	Thursday	Saturday	Friday
Dragon	Sunday	Wednesday	Thursday
Horse/Snake	Tuesday	Friday	Wednesday
Sheep	Friday	Monday	Thursday
Bird/Monkey	Friday	Thursday	Tuesday
Dog	Monday	Wednesday	Thursday

"All good fortune and all suffering without exception arises from the activities of the elements-this is why the calculations are important."

– Philippe Cornu

The Nine sMeba (Mewas):

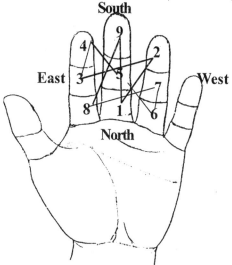

Figure 5 A: Position of sMeba

sMeba literally means mole or black spot which appears on our body . The astrology of the sMeba is based upon a system of 9 numbers, inscribed upon a magic square on the belly of the Turtle Manjushri. It is therefore oriented with regard to Space: the yellow 5 is in the Center, the white 6 at the Northwest, the red 7 at the West, the white 8 at the Northeast, the red 9 at the South, the white 1 at the North, the black 2 at the Southwest, the blue 3 at the East, the green 4 at the Southeast.

All the nine sMeba have a specific colour; 1, 6, 8 are White, being symbolical of the element of Metal; black for 2, and blue for 3 sMeba represents the element of Water, while the 4 which is green, represents wood and the 5 figure being yellow represents the element of Earth; the 7th and 9th sMeba represent the element of fire. Among the sMeba, the black "2" is the strongest or powerful one. Each year is not only related to an animal sign, but also sMeba and Parkha. If someone born in this sMeba normally may become famous if they work hard.

The nine magic square numbers (nine sMeba) are arranged in the form of a quadratic square or circle, and the figures usually, in a magic square, such that the sum of squares is the same in all directions.

Each of the number arrangements is arranged in a pattern particular to it. Each number is associated with a particular colour, element and Parkha.

sMeba, symbolised by the numbers from 1 to 9, which appears from the nine orifices (bu kha dgu) of the turtle. The white 1 appears from the white cloud of the right eye, the black 2 appears from the black apple of the left eye, the blue 3 appears from the vapour of the mouth, the green 4 appears from the vapour of the genital part, the yellow 5 appears from the five drop serum of the right nose, the white 6 appears from the right ear, the red 7 appears from the blood of the left ear, the white 8 appears from the left nose and the red 9 appears from the buttock. It can be calculated only by number, one being the base or starting point of all numbers, while 9 is their extreme limit. Beyond 9 is zero and in order to begin counting again one has to start again from one in order to obtain 11, 12, 13 etc on to infinity.

Yearly sMeba will always decrease in order of the numbers. Let's say the sMeba of this year (2002) is "7" and next year is "6", in the year 2004 year, the yearly sMeba will be "5". The sMeba black 2, the yellow 5, and the white 8 are always ruled by the four strongest animal signs (Raba bzhi) which are Tiger, Monkey, Pig and Snake. The white 1, the green 4 and the red 7 are ruled by the four middle animal signs ('bringpo bzhi) are Mouse, Horse, Bird, and Rabbit (Hare). The blue 3, the white 6, and the red 9 are ruled by the four Poor signs (Thachung bzhi) are Ox, Sheep, Dog, and Dragon.

There are one hundred and eighty years cycle subdivided in to three sixty years cycles. Combining each sMeba with each of the years of the sixty years cycle (Logan

dugchu) result in the combination of twelve years cycles
with the five elements.

The 1st metreng starts from the sMeba white 1 (Wood
Mouse), counting backward ends at the sMeba yellow
5 (Water Pig) after sixty years. (sMe phreng gong mai
gchig dkar nas drug chu grans ldong lnnga ru sad).
The 2nd metreng starts from the green 4 sMeba and
ends at the white 8 (De nas bar pai bzhi la brgongs brgyad
zad) and the last metreng start with the red 7, and after
180 years ends with sMeba black 2 (sMe phreng vog
mai bdun la 'khor de yi tha ma gnyis su zad).

Each person also has a life force sMeba, body sMeba,
power sMeba, and luck sMeba. Before finding your life
force sMeba, you must be sure of your birth sMeba.
The birth sMeba is the same as the body sMeba.

Calculation of life force sMeba (srog sme):

Always start from one's birth sMeba and go four sMeba
ahead from it. That is your life force sMeba.
For example, if your birth sMeba is 4 then your life force
sMeba is 1.

1 2 3 **4** 5 6 7 8 9

Power or Wealth sMeba (dbang sme):

The power sMeba can be obtained by counting four places forward from your birth sMeba.

1 2 3 **4** 5 6 **7** 8 9

———————➤

Example: If your birth sMeba is green 4, count from it and stop at four that is red 7. Therefore red 7 is your power sMeba.

Table no. 18
Life force sMeba & Power sMeba
from the Birth sMeba

Life force sMeba	7	8	9	1	2	3	4	5	6
Body sMeba	**1**	**2**	**3**	**4**	**5**	**6**	**7**	**8**	**9**
Power sMeba	4	5	6	7	8	9	1	2	3

Luck sMeba (klung sme):

While finding the one's luck sMeba, it is quite complicated. The luck sMeba corresponds to the life force sMeba of the luck sign appropriate for any of the

131

four groups of three compatible year signs. For easiest way, you are advised to use the tables which is given below.

Example: If you are born in the 1st metreng, first look at your animal sign column and come down to the metreng the number which is given below is your luck sMeba.

Table no. 19
Luck sMeba

Deity of luck	Metal Monkey	Fire Snake	Water Pig	Wood Tiger
Animal Sign of concerned person	**Tiger, Horse, Dog**	**Pig, Sheep, Rabbit**	**Bird, Ox, Snake**	**Mouse, Dragon, Monkey**
1st Metreng 1864-1923	8	2	5	5
2nd Metreng 1924-1983	2	5	8	8
3rd Metreng 1984-2043	5	8	2	2

Calculation of the Birth sMeba:

To determine the birth sMeba, one should always place the sMeba of the present year or current sMeba at the centre.

Let's say this year 2002, the sMeba is "7" at the centre and 8 at Northwest, 9 at West, 1 at Northeast, 2 at South, 3 North, 4 Southwest, 5 East and 6 Southeast. The way of finding this method is called flying bird (bya phur gros).

On the completion of one circuit the calculation return to the center and so on until the desired magic square number (sMeba) corresponding to the concerned person's current age is ultimately obtained. This means that one can conveniently count the ages 1, 10, 19, 28, 37, 46, 55, 64, 73, 82, 91 and 100 years serially in the central sector and go upto your age that is your birth sMeba.

For instance, if you are born in the year 1978, and your age is 25 years old. Look at the above year and take any number which is nearest and smaller than your age. So let's take "19" and place it at the center (current year sMeba i.e. "7", 20 at 8, 21-9, 22-1, 23-2, 24-3, 25-4 So your birth sMeba is Green "4.

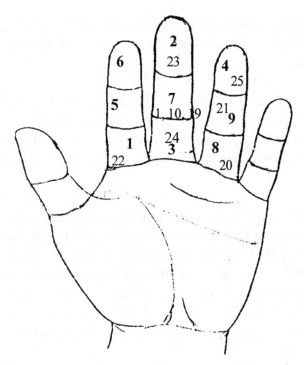

Figure 5 B: Calculation of birth sMeba

Current Year sMeba →

Ages of concerned person											Birth sMeba								
											1	**2**	**3**	**4**	**5**	**6**	**7**	**8**	**9**
1	10	19	28	37	46	55	64	73	82	91	1	2	3	4	5	6	7	8	9
2	11	20	29	38	47	56	65	74	83	92	2	3	4	5	6	7	8	9	1
3	12	21	30	39	48	57	66	75	84	93	3	4	5	6	7	8	9	1	
4	13	22	31	40	49	58	67	76	85	94	4	5	6	7	8	9	1	2	3
5	14	23	32	41	50	59	68	77	86	95	5	6	7	8	9	1	2	3	4
6	15	24	33	42	51	60	69	78	87	96	6	7	8	9	1	2	3	4	5
7	16	25	34	43	52	61	70	79	88	97	7	8	9	1	2	3	4	5	6
8	17	26	35	44	53	62	71	80	89	98	8	9	1	2	3	4	5	6	7
9	18	27	36	45	54	63	72	81	90	99	9	1	2	3	4	5	6	7	8

Table no. 20
Birth sMeba

Calculation of Changeable sMeba (babs sme):

It is important to clearly understand one's birth sMeba and keep it at the centre. At the beginning of the count, in the case of person born in one of the six male years sign (Mouse, Tiger, Dragon, Horse, Monkey, Dog), one moves directly east from the centre and then continues in an anti-clock wise sequence. In the case of persons born in one of the six female years sign (Ox, Rabbit, Snake, Sheep, Bird, Pig), go clockwise and stop at your age.

Let's do an example of a person who was born in 1978 and 25 years old. Always place your birth sMeba which is Green "4" at the center, 5 at Northwest, 6 at West, 7 at Northeast, 8 at South, 9 at North, 1 at Southwest, 2 at East, 3 at Southeast then put 1, 10, 19 at the center and exit from the East direction, and going anti-clockwise (Northeast, downward) stop at your age. So your changeable sMeba is "1" in this year.

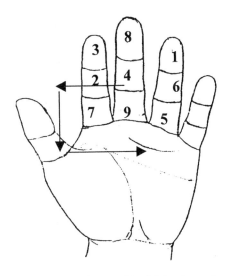

Figure 5 C: Changeable sMeba for male

If the animal sign of concerned person is female:

Do the same as before but go clockwise (upward, Southeast and stop at your age. That is your changeable sMeba. Changeable sMeba is useful especially when someone has died. One can make a statue by finding one's changeable sMeba and also for other interpretation.

For example, a 36 year old who was born in the year 1967 and animal sign is Fire Sheep.
Put 1, 10, 19, 28 as her birth sMeba i.e. White "6" at the center, 29-4, 30-5. 31-1, 32-3, 33-8, 34-7, 35-2, 36-9. So your changeable sMeba is Red "9".

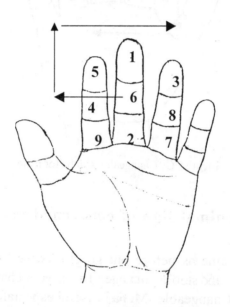

Figure 5 D: Changeable sMeba for female

Secrets of Determining Your Birth sMeba (skyes sme):

Current year sMeba (gnam sme) means the ruling sMeba of the particular year. So a person born in that particular year is ruled by that sMeba. Lets say, the ruling sMeba of this year '2002' is sMeba number "7". Therefore, the sMeba number "7" becomes the birth sMeba of any person who is born in this year. The sMeba of the year (gnam sme)-2002, always find in decreasing order number. As we know that the sMeba of this year is "7", so next year is "6", in the year 2004 the sMeba is 5, then 4, then 3, 2 and 1. After 1 then back to 9.

In the Elemental Astrological Text "Jung tsee man ngag zla ba'i 'od zer", it is mentioned that to find out one's birth sMeba, first one has to know the current sMeba of the year (when you do calculation), and then start the calculation. It is clear that without knowing the current year sMeba (gnam sme), one cannot find one's birth sMeba (skyes sme) easily.

So here I am telling you how to find the birth sMeba (skyes sme) without going through a long process to find it.

First of all, we have to classify the year into two groups.

1) The year up to Y2k (1900-2000)
2) The year after Y2k (2001——)
Up to the year 2000, always substract from "10", and from the year 2001 subtract from "9".

So using this calculation we either have to memorize the sMeba of the year or just know the previous sMeba. Then we automatically find the next number. Let's say the previous sMeba number of the year (2001) is "8". So this year is "7".

Let's say if someone was born in 1978, take the last two digit number 78, add those two digits i.e. 7+8=15, add again and make it into one digit, 1+5=6. Now subtract this number from 10-6=4. So we have got the remainder Green "4" which is his or her birth sMeba (skyes sme) easily.

E.g. for 2002, take the last two digits which are 0+2=2. Subtract this number from 9, so we get the sMeba number Red "7". A person born in this year is ruled by sMeba number Red "7". The Red 7 is his or her birth sMeba.

How to Read Your Past and Future Lives?
(Interpretation of the Mewas)

གཅིག་དཀར

White 1 Metal -gchig dkar
(The mirror of medicine)

Character: A Person born in this sMeba is kind hearted, honest, sharp minded, loves to travel, but has a short temper and is slow by nature. These people are egotistical and rarely achieve their wishes. They normally experience sorrow and stress in early life but happiness in their later life. They possess cleanliness and fond of working.

Past life: You were born as a son of a God in your past life.

Next life: You will probably be born as a bird or goat in the next life. If you consecrate a statue or build a thangka of lord Avalokiteshvara (chenrezig) and collect maximum virtue deeds in this life, you may be reborn as a God or Brahman in your next life. You will be born with a birthmark or black mole on the lower part of your body.

141

གཉིས་ནག

Black 2 Water- gnyis nag
(The mirror of devil)

Character: You will normally enjoy good health, though you may suffer from a particular illness you can easily recover from. You may experience early separation from your relatives. You are rough by nature, will face wealth deprivation, and are soft spoken. You are a bit egotistic; and fond of non-veg. foods.

Past life: You were born as a son of a devil. As a sign of your past life, you are nice and gentle spoken but inside you are a strong character in this life.

Next life: You will probably be born as a monkey in the next life. If you consecrate a statue or build a thangka of lord Vajrapani (chakdo) in this life, you will surely be reborn as a religious man in your next life. As a mark, you will have a mole on your ribs, hand, or neck.

གསུམ་མཐིང

Blue 3 Water-gsum mthing
(The mirror of ocean medicine)

Character: A person born in this sMeba is a bit jealous, egotistical, stingy, cunning, and changeable by nature. You love to do things particularly your way and hardly listen to others. You will be love by higher people, and lower people will dislike you. You are ambitious and difficult to satisfy. You are kind to others. You will be prevented from attaining higher positions of power in life, and this will very well disappoint you.

Past life: In your past live, you were born as an Elephant. As a sign, you are fond of sleeping and have a brave heart.

Next life: You will probably be born as a elephant in the next life. If you consecrate a statue or build a thangka of lord Vajrasattva (dorje sempa) and give alms and recite a hundred thousand syllable (yig gya) in this life. You will surely be reborn as a female in the west to a rich family in your next life. You will be born with a birthmark or black mole on your shoulder or ribs.

143

 བཞི་ལྗང

Green 4 Wood-bzhi ljang
(The mirror of Naga)

Character: Short tempered, good wealth, clear speech, sharp-minded, get hurt easily, clean, talkative, and love to help others. You love traveling and long walk. You do a good job but results will be claimed by others. You do not like to stay in a lower position, but others will interfere with your promotions. You are sensible, and articulate.

Past life: You were born as a Naga, then to the White deer.

Next life: You will probably be born as a cuckoo in the next life. If you consecrate a statue or build a thangka of Lord Vajrapani (chakdor) and make one hundred thousand stamp clays (tsa tsa) in this life, you will be reborn as a Tantric practitioner in your next life. To show that you have a mole or birth mark on right hand and face.

ལྔ་སེར

Yellow 5 Earth-lnga ser
(The mirror of the war-god)

Character: Intelligent, egotistical, faithful, kindhearted, honest by nature. You are a powerful speaker, highly ambitious and difficult to satisfy.

Past life: You were born as a sage in your previous life.

Next life: You will probably be born as a monkey or home bird in the next life. If you consecrate a statue or build a thangka of Lord Buddha (Tonpa) in this life, you will be reborn as a male religious practitioner or tantrician in your next life.

དྲུག་དཀར

White 6 Metal-drug dkar
(The mirror of King)

Character: You love to walk or travel on spare time and never tell lie. You enjoy good health, are seldom sick and often experience financial deprivations. If you worship a wealth deity you may increase your wealth and property. You are gifted with a superior intellect but have an unstable mind.

Past life: In your previous live, you were a God.

Next life: You will probably be born as a bird in the next life. If you consecrate a statue or build a thangka of Lord Vijaya (zug tor) in this life, you may be, reborn in the south as an educator in your next life.

བདུན་དམར

Red 7 Fire-bdun dmar
(The mirror of Mount dwelling spirit)

Character: You love non-vegetarian food and experience conflict with others. You are bit nervous and forgetful. You are a brave hearted and skillful. You may receive blames without reason and you yourself will be escaping from your work. But where there is food, you will be there. You have a strong digestion power.

Past life: You were born as a mount dwelling spirit or semi-god.

Next life: You will probably be born as a wolf in the next life. If you consecrate a statue or build a thangka of goddess Tara (dolma) in this life, you may reborn as a male in your next life. As proof you will be born with a birthmark or black mole on your chest, ribs, or hand.

བརྒྱད་དཀར

White 8 White-brgyad dkar
(The mirror of country god)

Character: You will be loved by higher people, and lower people will dislike you. You will enjoy happiness in your whole life if you collect maximum virtuous deeds and avoid all sinful activities. You will have good health and more happiness in your later life. You are slow, profound and little talkative, but inside you are hard. You have a white complexion, sharp nose and a big ego. You often receive respect from other people. Your ailments will be easily cured. You are good at handicrafts, intelligent, and possess a sharp mind. You are well educated and are devoted to a spiritual life.

Past life: In your past live, you were born as a son of a god.

Next life: You will probably be born as a female in the next life. If you consecrate a statue or build a thangka of Lord Buddha (tonpa) in this life, you will surely be reborn as a thangka painter in your next life.

དགུ་དམར

Red 9 Fire-dgu dmar
(The mirror of prosperity)

Character: You can collect good wealth but are bit stingy by nature. You neither spend your wealth yourself nor give to others. You will be happy in the later part of your life. Noble people will love you, but lower people will dislike you. You are open-minded but are a bit jealous and have a strong desire for material possessions, particularly property.

Past life: You were born as a dog to a rich family.

Next life: You will probably be reborn as a dog in the next life. If you consecrate a statue or build a thangka of lord Manjushri (Jampel yang) and collect maximum virtue deeds in this life, you may be reborn as male in your next life. As a sign, you will have a black mole or birthmark on your face, neck, head, or leg.

The Eight Parkhas

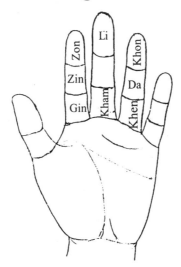

Figure 6 A: Position of Parkha

The Tibetan term Parkha is probably derived from the Chinese pa-kwa, the trigrams which are also formed as the basis for I-ching divination. The eight parkha appears from the eight aggregate consciousness of the turtle. Li from the Eye, Khon from root consciousness (kun gzhi), Da from emotion (nyon mongs), Khen from the mind, Kham from the tongue, Gin from the body, Zin from the ear, Zon from the nose.

149

In Chinese Pa means eight, and kha is the symbol used for divining by means of the 8 famous trigrams.

This system consists of eight trigrams that represent the elements, the directions and the seasons. They are depicted in the Tibetan system, as in the Chinese system, as combinations of broken and unbroken lines.

Although the Parkha in the Tibetan system are similar in meaning to those in the Chinese system, the Tibetans use the Parkha mostly in astrological determinations that are arrived at by mathematical calculations. The parkha is not commonly used in Tibet for divination using sticks or coins, as has been popular in China. Every person has a particular parkha that influences them.

The eight diagrams or parkha are represented by the name of elements. Each of nine sMeba numbers corresponds to a trigram. According to Tibetan Astrology, all matter on Earth is composed of five elements: Wood, Fire, Earth, Metal and Water. These elements can be further classified either into seven or eight elements. Wood, Fire, Earth, Water, Metal, Space, Wind, and Mountain. When we add the earth element to the above list, the number of elements becomes eight. The process of bringing together these eight into five elements involves combining Space and Metal; likewise,

150

Wind with Wood and Mountain falls under the Earth element. However, in this system parkha, Space Mountain and Wind are brought under the earth element (due to the actual position of the eight elements).

The trigram consists of three lines and it is given in figure. Individually they are named, Earth, Metal, Space, Water, Fire, Mountain, Wood, and Wind.

SOUTH: The number is 9, and South corresponds to the fire element. Its trigram is called LI

NORTH: The number is 1, and North corresponds to the water element. Its trigram is KHAM

EAST: The number is 3, and East corresponds to the Wood element and trigram is ZIN

WEST: The number is 7, and West corresponds to the metal element. Its trigam is Da.

The Intermediate points contain the numbers 2, 4, 6 and 8 which are corresponds to four different aspects of the element Earth (Earth, Sky, Mountain, Wood) Kon, Khen, Zon and Zin.

Positive and Negative Directions of the Parkha:

Parkha can be divided into eight areas: four favorable and four unfavorable. It is used to determine an individual's good and bad directions each year according to one's changeable parkha.

The four favourable or positive directions are:

Sky Medicine (gnam sman)

Life support (srog 'tsho)

Prosperity (dpal skyed)

Message of luck (phya lon)

The four unfavourable or negative directions are:

Injury (gnod pa)

Five Demons ('dre lnga)

Life cutting demons (bdud gcod)

Piece of body (lus chad).

The Sky Medicine (gnam sman) direction: It is very favourable for inviting doctors and medical procedures, etc.

The Life Support (srog 'tsho) direction: It is advised that the head of the bed should be expose in this direction, specifically when some one feels uncomfortable while sleeping or when someone falls sick. The symbol of this direction is a Mirror.

The Prosperity (dpal skyed) direction favours good luck and for earning wealth fortune. The symbol is Knot of eternity.

The Message of Luck (phya lon) direction is a good omen for undertaking a journey. The symbol is Triangle.

The Injury (gnod pa), direction is one to be avoided. Otherwise one may encounter an accident. The symbol is Triangle.

For the Five Demons ('dre lnga) direction, the symbol is five dots or points. It is advised to display a diagram of ransom (lue) in this direction, which represents the individual and his goods in order to deceive the demons.

The Life Cutting Demons (bdud gcod) direction: It is important for performing religious events in combating evil spirits. The symbol is a ritual dagger.

The Pieces of Body (lus chad) direction: In this direction one can recall one's lost bla (soul). The symbol is body parts.

Determining Your Personal Parkha:

The calculation of a person's birth Parkha is not too complicated, but you must be certain of your mother's age. Subtract your age from your mother's age, and add one to the remainder and then divide this number "8". Keep the remain
der number for calculation. Starting always from Parkha Kham (5th parkha), count counterclockwise until you reach the number you ended up with in calculation above. This is your birth Parkha.

For instances, if your mother is 58 years old and your age is 28.

$$
\begin{array}{r}
58 \\
- 28 \\
\hline
30 \\
+ 1 \\
\hline
31 \\
\div 8 \\
\hline
7 \\
\end{array}
$$
(Remainder number after dividing by 8)

Put always 1 on Kham, 2-Khen, 3-Da, 4-Khon, 5-Li, 6-Zon, 7-Zin. Therefore his/her birth Parkha is Zin.
If you want to do rapid calculation then put always 1 on kham, 10-khen, 20-khon, 30-Zon, 40-Gin, khen-50, etc.
So use the same knowledge and do the rest.

Changeable Parkha (babs spar):

A Changeable Parkha is a parkha or trigram, which changes each year.

Calculation:

To find out your changeable Parkha, one should note that the male and female will be differentiate by the concerned person. If the concerned person is male, one should count clockwise or downward starting from Li (li, khon, da, khen, kham, gin, zin, zon) and stopping at your age. Whereas if the concerned person is female one should count anticlockwise or upward direction starting from Kham (kham,, khen, da, khon, li, zon, zin and gin). This is the same method as is used in the calculation of birth parkha.

According to the Elemental Astrology text ('byung rtis man ngag zla bai' vod zer)

"Chu kha ma long re re rtsi"
Chu ka long na zur kah chong"

While finding your parkha, at every ten count one can calculate by jumping right to the corners and at other digits are needs to count by going from each block. Eventually one will obtain the trigram corresponding to the concerned person's current age.

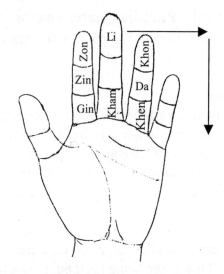

Figure 6 B: Changeable Parkha for male

Male:

For example, 70 years old man. Put one at Parkha Li
(starting point) and then put at the corner always, 10-
khon, 20-Khen, 30-Gin, 40-Zon, 50-Khon, 60-Khen
and 70-Gin etc. Thus, his babs par or changeable Parkha
is Gin.

Take another example, if someone is 29 years old male
and his animal sign is Tiger. Do the same method as
above upto the 20 and then go one by one. Put 1-li, 10-
Khon, 20-Khen, 21-Kham, 22-Gin, 23-Zin, 24-Zon,
25-Li, 26-Khon, 27-Da, 28-Khen and 29-kham.

So the Kham is his babs par or changeable parkha this year.

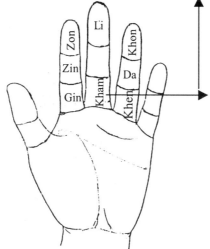

Figure 6 C: Changeable Parkha for female

Female:

Example: A female born in 1985 and is 18 years old. Place 1 on Kham, 10 on Khen, 11 on Da, 12 on Khon, 13 on Li, 14 on Zon, 15 on Zin, 16 on Gin, 17 on Kham, 18 on Khen. Thus, her bab spar is Khen this year.

Another example:

If someone is 80 years old. Always put 1 on Kham, 10-Khen, 20-Khon, 30-Zon, 40-Gin, 50-Khen, 60-Khon, 70-Zon, and 80-Gin, etc. Therefore Gin is her changeable parkha this year.

Interpretation of the Parkhas:

Li

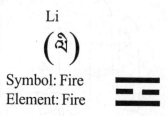

Symbol: Fire
Element: Fire

Li consists of a broken line between two unbroken lines. It is in the South position and relates to the youngest daughter. The element of Li is Fire. It also relates to summer.

Characteristics:
A person born in this parkha usually loves to tell lies, suffers from headaches, and is soft spoken by nature. You are loved by the higher people and lower people dislike you. You will frequently experience wealth deprivation. You may be harmed by the Nagas. You are likely to die under the knife.

Khon

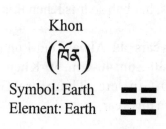

Symbol: Earth
Element: Earth

158

Khon is made of three broken lines. It is in the southwest position and relates to the mother. The animal associated with it is the Sheep, and the element of Khon is Earth. It represents the end summer.

Characteristics:
You are intelligent, soft spoken but rough inside. Love to backbite to others. You will live a long life, however, you will often experience suffering and illness throughout your life. You will have many daughters. You are often visibly moody and will face financial ups and downs. You may die from cancer, defilements and dropsy (smu chu). You will be rich in early life and poor in later life. You will constantly be consumed by hatred, it will be difficult for you to raise children, and there will be divorce or widowhood.

Da

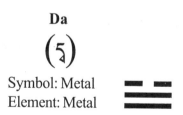

Symbol: Metal
Element: Metal

Da consists of two unbroken lines beneath a broken line. It is in the west and relates to the middle son. The element of Da is Metal, and the animals associated with it are the

Bird and Monkey. Da relates to autumn.

Characteristics:
Talkative by nature, broad- minded. Prefer to perform virtuous deeds in this life. You are well educated, and will have around four children. You may die from a kidney disease or disorder. You will experience wealth fluctuation. You are kind hearted, bold, strong and get hurt easily. You possess little guile but much ferocity, bravery and self-sufficiency.

Khen

Symbol: Heaven
Element: Earth

Khen consists of three unbroken lines. It is in the northwest position and relates to the head of the family, usually the father. It represents heaven and the element of Khen is earth. The animal associated with it is the dog. It represents the end of autumn.

Characteristics:
You love to debate, but you are a tolerant person. You may have to experience stress and are likely to suffer

160

from Elephantiasis (rkang bam). You will be arrogant and proud. You will skillfully assess the wealth of others and will experience few joys.

Kham

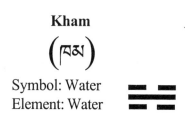

Symbol: Water
Element: Water

Kham is made up of one unbroken line between two broken lines. It is placed in the north position and relates to the youngest son. The element of Kham is water, and the animals associated with it are the Mouse and Pig. Kham represents winter.

Characteristics:
You have a strong affectionate towards family, but you are harsh to others. You are internally stubborn but loved by the higher people. You may experience weakness in your kidneys. You will be aloof and self-determining.

Gin

(གིན་)

Symbol: Mountain
Element: Earth

Gin consists of two broken lines beneath an unbroken
line. It is in the northeast position and relates to the eldest
son. The animal associated with it is Ox, and the element
is Mountain (Earth). It relates to late winter.

Characteristics:
You hardly receive help from others, and you will face
difficulty in raising your children. You are a romantic.
People enjoy being in your presence. You prefer simple
and minor work. You may experience financial deprivation.
You will be heavily built quiet and steadfast in word.

Zin

(ཟིན་)

Symbol: Wood
Element: Wood

Zin is made up of two broken lines above an unbroken line.
It is in the east position and represents the middle daughter.

162

The element of zin is wood and the animals associated with it are the Tiger and Rabbit. It represents spring.

Characteristics:
Rough behaviour within your family but gentle outside. You may have one to three children. You will have a slightly blue colored complexion. You may suffer from joint pain in the hands or feet, and will be harmed by the devil or Landlord evil spirits. You may be poor in your earlier life and will enjoy good wealth and happy in your later life. You will come to possess children and wealth, despite your rough speech and domestic losses.

Zon

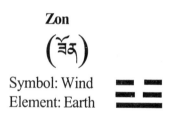

Symbol: Wind
Element: Earth

Zon consists of one broken lines beneath two unbroken lines. It is in the southeast position and relates to the eldest daughter. It relates to late spring.

Characteristic:
You will greatly esteem both mental and physical activities. You may hold two different countries. You are a strong

163

attachment and have many mental works. You will have a great contention and often experience ups and downs in your financial status.

> *"The Wheel of Time establishes a correspondence*
> *between the macrocosm and microcosm in*
> *terms of the formation of the universe and fetal*
> *development, and between the configuration*
> *of the universe and the shape and*
> *size of the human body."*
> **—Jamgon Kongtrul Lodro Taye**

The Planets (gZa)

There are eight planets (gZa') in Elemental Astrology.

1) The sun (Nyi ma)
2) The moon (Dawa)
3) Mars (Migmar)
4) Mercury (Lhakpa)
5) Jupiter (Phurbu)
6) Venus (Pasang)
7) Saturn (Penpa)
8) Rahu/moon node (Dachen)

The seven weekdays (res gza) are

Sunday

Monday

Tuesday

Wednesday

Thursday

Friday

Saturday

The different days of the week are associated with the elements; thus Sunday and Tuesday are associated with the fire element and are present in the South Direction.
Monday and Wednesday are Water element and present in the North
Thursday is Wood element and present in the East direction.

Friday is Metal element and present in the West direction. Saturday is the earth element and present in all the four cardinal.

Rahu is present in all the directions and has the potency of all five elements.

The symbols of the days are: a Sun for Sunday, a crescent Moon for Monday, a red eye for Tuesday, a hand for Wednesday, a ritual dragger for Thursday, a Metal for Friday, a broom for Saturday, and a head of crows for Rahu (da chen)

"There is no doubt the astrological system based on the nine mewa numbers is a science characteristic of the ancient Bon tradition. In common usage the Tibetan word mewa (smeba) means 'mole', birthmark, and this is the etymological meaning underlying the astrological term. In fact, just as moles are unmistakable signs that remain throughout one's life in the same places on the body, the mewa are characteristic positive or negative signs that recur invariably and with periodic consistency during astrological time cycles."

Professor Namkhai Norbu Rinpoche

Significance of the Seven Weekdays:

ཉི་མ

Sunday (Nyima)

Person born on Sunday will gain love and favour from higher people. He or she will have fair complexion and are honest by nature.
Male: He is rich and will lead a luxurious life. By nature he is very decisive. He will lead a better, more comfortable life abroad.
Female: She is rich and will make a good housewife.

ཟླ་བ

Monday (Dawa)

A Person born on Monday will have a white complexion, will be tall in stature, and is cunning. They will often receive love and care from others. They will experience financial ups and downs.
Male: He is wealthy and powerful.
Female: She is beautiful, sincere, and attractive.

 མིག་དམར

Tuesday (Migmar)

A Person born on Tuesday will perform sinful activities and will have a short temperament. They possess strong hatred towards others and have a red complexion. They are divisive and egoistical.

Male: He will face problems as in his grow up.

Female: She will have a short life span.

ལྷག་པ

Wednesday (Lhakpa)

A Person born on Wednesday will often face health problem. They are sharp-minded, kind hearted, short tempered and possess a dark complexion. Delay in their work is the main draw back of a person born on Wednesday. They are straightforward. Blue colour clothing and green vegetables are good or suitable for them.

Male: Their mother will experience certain hindrances in their life.

Female: Decline in parent's wealth, but she will become rich and powerful.

ཕུར་བུ

Thursday (Phurbu)

A Person born on Thursday is gifted with a strong intelligent and is religious by nature. They have a red complexion, are violent, and will experience ups and downs in their life. They will gain property from others.
Male: He is quick witted, handsome, good looking, and well educated.
Female: She will live a long life span and have a good husband and friends.

པ་སངས

Friday (Pasang)

A Person born on Friday will have a fair complexion and will be loved by their teacher. They involve in business, and hot and bile disorders are likely to come into their life. White colour of beverages, foods, clothes are suitable for them.
Male: He will live a long life span and is highly intelligent.
Female: She may often face illnesses, but she will have prosperity.

སྤེན་པ

Saturday (Penpa)

A Person born on Saturday will have a good figure but
have less fortune. They will be love by their teacher and
higher people. They are intelligent and may live abroad.
Male: Life span will be medium.
Female: Short life span.

*"The Internal Kalachakra and Tibetan Medical
texts share many similarities regarding
the mode of treatment, remedial measures, rites
and rituals, medicines, behavioural guidelines,
yogic practice etc. Both the texts emphasize and
hold the same view, regarding the formation
of the human body, disease as an expression of
imbalance among the elements and the
corresponding treatment which should be
composed by the same elemental substances."*
—Dr. Tsering Thakchoe Drungtso

Do You Want to Know Your Birth Weekday (skyes gza)?

People may know their date of birth (year/month/date/ time), but may not know or remember, the day (gza) when they were born. Since it is extremely important to know one's day of birth, here reveals the secret of determining one's weekday. In general you may probably use a Tibetan Astrological almanac or ephemeris to confirm the day of the week you were born. However, if you want to know yourself without need to consult almanac or ephemeris, here is the short cut method to find out your birthday (gza) in a minute.

Table no. 21: Year

1	2	3	4	5	6	7	8	9
2000	2001	1935	1924	1931	1926	1927	1933	1928
		1940	1930	1936	1937	1932	1939	1934
		1946	1941	1942	1943	1938	1944	1945
		1957	1947	1953	1948	1949	1950	1951
		1963	1952	1959	1954	1955	1961	1956
		1968	1958	1964	1965	1960	1967	1962
		1974	1969	1970	1971	1966	1972	1973
		1985	1975	1981	1976	1977	1978	1979
		1991	1980	1987	1982	1983	1989	1984
		2002	1986	1992	1993	1988	1995	1990

171

Table no. 22: Month

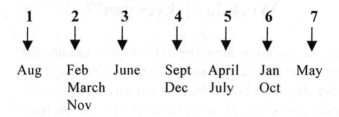

1	2	3	4	5	6	7
Aug	Feb March Nov	June	Sept Dec	April July	Jan Oct	May

Weekdays: The seven weekdays are numbered from 0 to 6.

0 for **Saturday (Penpa)**
1 for **Sunday (Nyima)**
2 for **Monday (Dawa)**
3 for **Tuesday (Migmar)**
4 for **Wednesday (Lhakpa)**
5 for **Thursday (Phurbu)**
6 for **Friday (Passang)**

An Example:

Find out the weekday of a person who was born on 29th May 1990
First of all, look at the table of the year which we got "9" for the year 1990   **9**

172

Then find the month which is May
(look at the month table) we got "7"   7
Lastly add the date "29" to the year   29
and month which is(9+7+29).   _____
                                                                45
                                                      ===========

Now, divide the total number (45) by 7, we got 6 as quotient and 3 as remainder.

Always use the remainder to get your weekday. So, the remainder is 3, which is Tuesday. Therefore you were born on Tuesday (Migmar).

Take one more example:
A person born on 3rd March 1974. Find his birth weekday?

First look at the table of the year and month. Then add the date with the year and month.

1974	**3**
March	**2**
Date (3rd)	**3**
Total	= 8

Divided by 7, 8:-7=1, so the weekday is Sunday (Nyima) or you were born on Sunday.

Note:

Generally you have "2" for February and "6" for January. Do not use the above method in the leap year. Here is the numbers, which you could use only in the leap year. For **February,** it is 1and for **January** it is **5.**

"One simple way of viewing the philosophy behind astrology is through understanding the influence of the basic elements of nature. This is only one aspect of astrology, and many other factors are involved, but this description gives a partial idea of how astrology works."
—**Tai Situpa Rinpoche**

Constellations and it's interpretation

The twenty seven constellations are considered in astrological calculations to predict the outcoming. The constellation bro zhin and byi zhin are both situated in one star cluster; however they may be counted separately to make twenty eight.

East and wood element constellations are smin drug, snar ma, mgo, lag, nabs so, rgyal

South and fire element constellations are mchu, bre, dbo, me gzhi, nag pa, sari

North and water element constellations are lha mtsams, snron, snrubs, chu stod, chu smad, gro zhin

West and Metal element constellations are mon gre, mon gru, khrums stod, khrum smad, nam gru, tha skar

The four cardinal (Southeast, Southwest, Northwest and Northeast) and earth element constellations are skag, saga, byi zhin, bra nye respectively.

The Twenty-seven constellations are:
1) Tha kar (tha skar)
2) Da nye (dra nye)
3) Min duk (smin drug)
4) Narma (snar ma)
5) Go (mgo)
6) Lak (lag)

7) Nab so (nabs so)
8) Gyal (rgyal)
9) Kak (skag)
10) Chu (mchu)
11) Dey (bre)
12) Wo (dbo)
13) Me shi (me gzhi)
14) Nakpa (nag pa)
15) Sa ree (sari)
16) Saka (saga)
17) Lhatsam (lha mtsams)
18) Non (snron)
19) Nub (snrubs)
20) Chu toe (chu stod)
21) Chu mey (chu smad)
21) Do shin (gro bzhin)
22) Ji shin (byi bzhin)
23) Mon dey (mon gre)
24) Mon doo (mon gru)
25) Tum toe (khrums stod)
26) Tum mey (khrum smad)
27) Nam doo (nam gru)

ཐ་སྐར

0) Tha skar
Indian Name: Aswini
Western Name: Arietic

It has three stars shaped like the neck of a horse.
A person born in this constellation will have a sharp mind,
a good physical appearance, and religious by nature.
They are interested in dance, song, and music. They also
enjoy travelling.

Favourable:
Hoisting prayer flags, shifting cemetery to other, hair cut
and nails, performing peaceful activities, washing hair,
digging ponds, irrigation canals and wells.

Unfavourable:
Wearing nice ornaments, compounding medicine,
building houses, blood letting, moxabustion, giving bribes,
laying foundation of a house, sending infants to other
residences outside of the family.

ཟ་ཉེ

1) Bra nye
Indian Name: Bharni
Western Name: Triangalara

It has three stars in the shape of the secret parts (sexual organs) of a female.

A person born in this constellation will have a stable mind, enjoy good health, be honest by nature, become an expert in arts and handicrafts, is kind hearted, and hard working.

Favourable:
Receiving initiations, raising prayer flags, naming of a child, buying of horses and other animals, helping widows.

Unfavourable:
Compounding medicinal herbs, blood letting, incense burning ceremony, planting trees, sending bribes, avoid doing virtuous deeds, building houses, sowing seeds and doing business, do both peaceful and productive activities.

སྨིན་དྲུག

2) sMin drug
Indian Name: Krittika
Western Name: Pleiades

It has six stars in the shape of a sharp knife.
A person born in this constellation will increase their
wealth and may become very learned. They are bold,
daring and will enjoy better conditions in later life.

Favourable:
To saddle horse, admitting to the monastery, burnt
offerings, giving alms to others, making medicine, wearing
ornaments, making stupa or temple, meeting with
relatives, horse racing ceremony, washing hair and
virtuous deeds.

Unfavourable:
Planting flowers and trees, working with buildings,
sending bribes, making water channels, sowing fields,
and hoisting prayer flags. Avoid working with dead
bodies, to suppress such an evil spirit.

 སྨར་མ

3) sNar ma
Indian Name: Rohini
Western Name: Aldebran

It has five stars in the shape of a chariot.
A person born in this constellation will live a long life, have an attractive body and beautiful, and bold hearted. You will triumph over your enemies. You may become wealthy and religious minded with a less evasive tendency.

Favourable:
Buying and selling things, blood letting, cutting hair and nails, peaceful activities, making medicine, receiving money and animals from others, constructing building and incense burning ceremonies.

Unfavourable:
Working with dead bodies, both sending and receiving bribes.

སྨྲོ

4) mGo
Indian Name: Mrigasira
Western Name: Orionis

It has three stars in the shape of head of a wild animal. A person born in this constellation is a religious person and always speaks the truth. They are bold with a clear mind and may become wealthy.

Favourable:
To suppress evil spirits (sri gnan), planting trees and flowers, make offering to the deity, commencing to build a new home, working in the field, wrathful activities, raising Buddhist banner, cutting nails and hair, to saddle horse and donkey, giving new name to a newly born child, doing business, horse racing ceremony, taking money.

Unfavourable:
Working with dead bodies or corpse, good for receiving bribe and bad for sending, sending money to outside.

ལག

5) Lag
Indian Name: Aridra
Western Name: Betelgeuse

It has one star in the shape of a drop (thigle) or zero.
A person born in this constellation is a bit egotistical.
You will come across many friends and colleagues around
you. You are interested in bad activities and may become
poor and stupid in general.

Favourable:
Becoming a monk, making divination, completing virtuous
deeds, washing hair, planting flowers and trees, digging
water channels and ponds, going to war. Suppressing
evil spirits and making request to higher people.

Unfavourable:
Making offerings to a deity, working with dead bodies,
moxabustion, raising prayer flags, peaceful and
auspicious activities.

ནབས་སོ

6) Nabso
Indian Name: Punarvasu
Western Name: Pollux

It has two stars in the shape of throne base
A person born in this constellation is well disciplined, has good financial status, is religious minded, enjoys good health, is stable minded but is a bit foolish by nature.

Favourable:
Incense burning ceremony, building temple, working with corpses, also the calling in of blessings. (If blessings are called in under this influence, you will become wealthy and prosperous (gyang 'gug). Burnt offering, Making medicine, studying, wiring, laying the foundation of buildings, making sand mandala, repaying loans, divination or astro. calculation of all types, blood letting and moxabustion, doing business, naming a child, sowing seeds in the field, receiving initiation and peaceful activities, to saddle horse and donkey.

Unfavourable:
Sending bribes is bad but receiving them is good. Sinful activities, spending money, destroying the house of deities, sending corpse.

ক্ৰুঅ

7) rGyal
Indian Name: pushyami
Western Name: Castor

It has three stars in the shape of a cylinder.

A person born in this constellation is religious minded, fond of giving alms to others, hard working, has a good figure, sharp minded, and interested in arts and handicrafts. You may become a scholar and have good wealth and property. But your mind and body are unstable.

Favourable:

Making mandala, receiving money and animals from others, giving names to children, wearing net-cloth, making irrigation canals, to saddle horse, compounding medicines, making divination, receiving initiation, and participating in peaceful and productive, and auspicious activities, and planting trees.

Unfavourable:

Attending to business matters, sowing seeds, in fields, to suppress such an evil spirit, construction work, washing hair, unfavourable sending bribes but favourable receiving them.

184

8) sKag
Indian Name: Aslesha
Western Name: Hydrae

It has six stars in the shape of the expanded hood of the cobra.

A person born in this constellation is a bit foolish by nature, but physically beautiful in appearance. You may have a shortlived relationship with your mother. You spend money lavishly. You have a short temper and are more interested in bad activities than good.

Favourable:
Going to war, repayment of loans, making irrigation channels and ponds, wrathful activities, planting trees.

Unfavourable:
Making divination, auspicious and virtuous deeds, receiving initiation as well as peaceful activities, sending corpse, construction, compounding medicines, both sending and receiving bribe.

ཨཆུ

9) mChu
Indian Name: Magha
Western Name: Regulas

It has six stars in the shape of a river.

A person born in this constellation loves telling lies. You may have lots of friends and enjoy good financial status. You are interested in craft arts You are a hard working person and interested in virtuous deeds.

Favourable:

Performing ritual cake puja, burnt offering, building temples, bloodletting, moxabustion, receiving money, purchasing horses and animals, studying, making sand mandala, cutting nails and hair, to suppress such an evil spirit, peaceful work, and looking for servant.

Unfavourable:

Building houses, washing hair, planting trees and flowers, raising prayer flags, making ponds and irrigation canals, saddling horses and donkeys, unfavourable for both sending and receiving bribes.

10) bre
Indian Name: Poorva Phalguni
Western Name: Zosma

It has two stars in the shape of human feet.
A person born in this constellation is evasive, stingy and desire driven. You love new clothes and love to wear ornaments. You are interested in crafts. You are soft spoken, clever, and love eating. You love gossiping with your friends.

Favourable:
Meeting with relatives, receiving wealth and animals, also initiation, making divination, incense burning ceremony, drawing mandala, burnt offering.

Unfavourable:
Raising Buddhist banner, bloodletting and moxabustion, sending animals and wealth to others, washing hair, making water channels, giving names, sending and receiving bribes are both bad.

11) dbo
Indian Name: Uttra Phalguni
Western Name: Denebala

It has two stars in the shape of a throne.
A person born in this constellation will become wealthy, loves to give alms, and is honest by nature. You love travelling or walking on your spare times. You can be foolish at times. You are a well-disciplined person.

Favourable:
Washing hair, meeting relatives, construction work, giving names, putting up Buddhist banner, virtuous activities, sending and receiving brides, peaceful activities, to saddle horse and donkey, making irrigation canals and ponds, sending money and property.

Unfavourable:
Farming, cutting nail and hair, planting flowers and trees, sending animals like yaks, goats and sheep.

ཨེ་བཞི

12) Me bzhi
Indian Name: Hast
Western Name: Corvas

It has five stars in the shape of a hand.
A person born in this constellation will have a well-built body, sharp tongue and an interest in arts. You love traveling and will have good wealth. You are evasive and sometimes too proud.

Favourable:
Cutting nails and hair, to saddle horse, donkey and mules, working on dead bodies, making buildings, compounding medicine, drawing sand mandala, farming, receiving initiation, both peaceful and wrathful activities.

Unfavourable:
Planting flowers and trees, sending yak and sheep outside, digging irrigation canal and ponds, receiving domestic animals from others, business, to build temple, handling with the corpse.

ནག་པ

13) Nagpa
Indian Name: Chitra
Western Name: Spica

It has one star in the shape of the heart of a lotus.
A person born in this constellation will be fond of song, dance and music. He /she will have a sharp tongue, possess intelligence and will speak the truth, but also be desire driven and indecisive or prone to changing his/her mind. You love to wear different clothes.

Favourable:
Washing hair, receiving money and domestic animals, compounding medicine, farming and sowing seeds, virtuous activities, religious teaching, and making mandalas.

Unfavourable:
Making irrigation canal and ponds, both peaceful and wrathful activities, giving names and sending bride.

ཤ་རེ

14) Sari
Indian Name: Swati
Western Name: Arcturus

It has one star in the shape of jewel.
A person born in this constellation will enjoy good wealth, have a beautiful face, and may be loved by high people and hated by lower people. He/she sometimes succumbs to jealously and is sometimes stingy. He/she will have an interest in composing poems and writing books.

Favourable:
To saddle horse, donkey and mules, taking back own house or place, venesection and moxabustion, to train riding animals like horse and ox, to build image of god or stupa, to propitiate a deity, gardening, burnt offering, meeting with relatives, farming, drawing mandala, sowing seed, recalling life, working with corpse, compounding medicine, suppressing evil spirit (sri gnan) and religious teaching.

Unfavourable:
Horse racing, shifting cemetery, beware of robbery and theft, constructing buildings, avoid wrathful activities.

ས་ག

15) Saga
Indian Name: Vaisakha
Western Name: Zubemubi

It has four stars in the shape of a goat head.
A person born in this constellation is majestic, has good wealth and will have many friends especially women in their life. You will enjoy better years in later life. You are an intelligent and capable of defeating opponents or enemies.

Favourable:
To construct a dam, to hold new house, involve in craft work, to enter sanga community, burnt offering, studying meeting relatives, receiving initiation, repaying loans, agriculture work, receiving bride but unfavourable sending a bride, to train horse and ox, cutting hair and nails.

Unfavourable:
Preparing medicine, both peaceful and productive activities, construction work, to build an image of god or temple, washing hair, creating a garden and planting flowers and trees, construct cemetery, divination.

ལྷ་མཚམས

16) Lha tsam
Indian Name: Anuradha
Western Name: Scorpius

It has four stars in the shape of an elephant.
A person born in this constellation has a sharp tongue, is well disciplined, possess a well-built body, and is intelligent and religious minded. He/she is an intellectual and fond of children.

Favourable:
To saddle horse and donkey, virtuous activities, to enter sanga community, cutting hair and nails, venesection and moxabustion, sowing seeds, washing hair and farming.

Unfavourable:
Construction work, to hold new house, subdue animals, to build town, peaceful activities, sending bride and suppressing evil spirit.

ཪྩོན

17) sNon
Indian Name: Jyeshtha
Western Name: Antares

It has four stars in the shape of a staircase.
A person born in this constellation is well disciplined, may become poor, interested in bad work, and will have a short life span.

Favourable:
Recalling life, to enter sanga community, construct bride, sowing seeds, sending horse outside, to make offering to deities, blood-letting and moxabution, planting trees.

Unfavourable:
Preparing medicine, divination, giving names, take back house or place, peaceful and productive activities, construction work, and both sending and receiving brides.

སྲུབས

18) sNubs
Indian Name: Moola
Western Name: Shaula

It has nine stars in the shape of a scorpion.
A person born in this constellation is a bit egotistical, and interested in bad activities.

Favourable:
Working with dead bodies, farming, building stupas and temples, business, making offering to gods, constructing building, taking wealth and property from others, ritual cakes, puja.

Unfavourable:
Raising Buddhist banner, giving names, burnt offering, to hold new house, both sending and receiving brides.

ཆུ་སྟོད

19) chu stod
Indian Name: Poorva shada
Western Name: Kaus-Aust

It has four stars in the shape of a stupa.
A person born in this constellation is a religious, and an

expert in handicrafts and all other kinds of work. He/
she is egotistical and will live a long life.

Favourable:
Washing hair, buying animals (like horse) and land,
constructing building, business, giving names, marriage
ceremony and sowing seeds.

Unfavourable:
Horse racing, working with corpse, peaceful and
productive activities, sending wealth to others, making
irrigation canals, and bad for the bride.

ཆུ་སྨད

20) Chu sMad
Indian Name: Uttra Shada
Western Name: Nunki

It has four stars in the shape of a grain measurer.
A person born in this constellation may become wealthy,
is honest, and loves to give alms to others. You will always
have many friends near by.

Favourable:
To build stupa and temple, construction work, saddle
horse, donkey and mules, making ponds and irrigation
canals, hoisting Buddhist banners, planting flowers and

trees, washing hair, doing auspicious work, making medicine, giving names, receiving initiation, sending and receiving bride and peaceful activities.

Unfavourable:
Sending animals like yak outside, wrathful activities, burning corpse, building cemeteries.

གྲོ་བཞིན

21) Gro bzhin
Indian Name: Sarvana
Western Name: Altair

It has three stars in the shape of a grain measurer.
A person born in this constellation is open minded, good hearted, loved by the higher people, bold, enjoys sound health, and will overcome enemies.

Favourable:
Farming, making irrigation canals and ponds, to hold new house, compounding medicines, making offerings to the deities, venesection, and moxabustion.

Unfavourable:
Receiving brides, entering the sanga community, repaying loans, suppressing evil spirits, peaceful activities, and working with dead bodies and trees.

བྱི་བཞིན

Byi bzhin

It has three stars in the shape of an ox head.
A person born in this constellation is broad minded,
educated, has few desires, kind hearted, wealthy and
bold by nature.

Favourable:
Cutting hair, making offerings to deities, and entering
sanga community.

Unfavourable:
Construction work, making Tibetan beer (chang), sowing
seeds, wrathful activities, divination, and working with
the dead body.

མོན་གྲེ

22) Mon gre
Indian Name: Dhamishta
Western Name: Delphinus

It has four stars in the shape of a bird.
A person born in this constellation is kind hearted, an
expert in medicine, wealthy, will have many children, hard

working, has a short temper, bad nature, fond of dancing and music, beautiful and gifted with a good figure, and lavish by nature.

Favourable:
To build temples, farming, preparing medicines, construction work, business, to hold new house, to make offering to deities, washing hair, and wrathful activities.

Unfavourable:
Horse racing, to saddle horse, donkey, and mew, working with corpse, sending wealth and animals outside.

ཨོན་གྲུ

23) Mon gru
Indian Name: Satbhisha
Western Name: Aquari

It has four stars in the shape of blown of a flower.
A person born in this constellation is wealthy, has a good figure, lives a lavish life, brave, healthy and hard working.

Favourable:
Compounding medicine, building temples, buying animals, planting trees.

Unfavourable:
Construction work, horse racing, cutting hair and nails,

making irrigations canals, both sending and receiving brides.

 འཁྲུམས་སྟོད

24) 'khrum stod
Indian Name: Poorva Bhadra
Western Name: Pegasus

It has two stars in the shape of a chariot.
A person born in this constellation is evasive, wealthy, is affectionate towards relatives, and stingy.

Favourable:
Giving names, virtuous activities, planting trees, preparing medicines, construction work, burnt offering ceremonies, offerings deities.

Unfavourable:
Making ponds and wells, washing hair, sending and receiving brides.

འཁྲུམས་སྨད

25) 'khrum sMad
Indian Name: Uttra Bhadra
Western Name: Pegas

It has two stars in the shape of an ear.
A person born in this constellation is fond of dancing and singing, religious minded, loves to help others, wealthy, honest by nature, well disciplined, intelligent and kind hearted. He/she enjoy circle of friends. He/she is capable of overcoming opponents and enemies.

Favourable:
Farming, making water channels, planting trees, washing hairs, preparing alcohol, and wrathful activities.

Unfavourable:
Construction work, making offerings to deities, bloodletting, and moxabustion, peaceful and productive activities.

ནམ་གྲུ

26) Nam gru
Indian Name: Rewati
Western Name: Piscium

It has thirty-two stars in the shape of a ship.
A person born in this constellation is good to others,
hard working and brave.

Favourable:
Wearing new clothes, construction work, preparing
medicines, virtuous activities, business, sowing seeds,
washing hair, working with corpses, giving names, cutting
nails and hair.

Unfavourable:
Going to war, sending out your wealth.

Tibetan Geomancy (Sachey)

The sources and propagation of Sachey:
Tibetan Geomancy examines the shape of the Earth, sky and formation of mountains, and predicts the rise and fall of individual households and countries.

The main importance of examining nature's strength is because all the substances are formed by the four elements and the different combinations of element either bring happiness or sorrow to the universe. All human beings are formed by the four elements. This knowledge is particular to Tibet and the Bon religion/culture. It often said that both the Macrocosm and microcosmic are formed from the element Egg.

In the year 755, Tibet king, Trisong Deutsen, was a proponent of Buddhism and is responsible for bringing the religion to Tibet. Tibetan Geomancy (sachey) was also introduced to Tibet around the same time. In 781, a Metal Ox year, Tibetan geomancy was used for the first time in helping construct the Samye temple.

Tibetan sachey is still practiced to this day for building temples, lay people's homes, stupas, cemeteries, etc. Tibetan geomancy is one of the old knowledge of ancient Tibet and it came due to the many changes of history related. The first Tibetan sachey came in the relation with Bon religion. Later it propagated in relation with Buddhism.

Sources:

The four Tibetan Earth observator (sa mkhan) went to Manasarowar Lake to learn the precious rosary teaching of sachey. They traveled with a white ox with black ear, which carried their luggage. Another ox appeared under the lake and both oxen started fighting. The ox from the lake was too strong, and Ma chig pelki Dorjee got angry and broke the ox's head with a stick, and then the ox jumped back into the lake. Later, a beautiful woman adorned with precious ornaments came out from the lake. Khyung goe Namkha ding asked her, "Who are you? Where are you going? "She replied, "I am a daughter of Naga King (tsug na Rinchen). Why did you break my ox's head? Why have you all come here? What do you want? Where are you going?" Khyunggoe Namkhading replied". We came here to learn the sand calculation, and we are sorry for breaking your ox's head. They requested the Nagi to teach the sand calculation. Nagi asked them, "What sort of offering have you brought? Khyungoe Namkhading replied, he has brought gold, Machig Pelgi Dorjee brought one ox, Sidpa Tulgee Miwo one gold like sheep size, Chongro Mitshar Tathing offered one horse. The Nagi was pleases with these gifts and told them to bring sand and pour it in front of her. So she taught sachey (sand calculation) in detail to them. In sachey, the father of earth is the sky, the mother of earth is earth, and the child of earth is atmosphere.

Importance of Sachey:
The elements of each person 's body are affected by the different elements of each country. For example, it is a general thing that people get hot disease etc due to the unsuitable element (water and earth), which brings different illness.

Particularly, the formation of each place and suitability of earth and sky.

The reason why we look for favorable and unfavorable cemetery is because according to the "chags med ri chos" the three life force, soul and consciousness. The life force is cut by the devil; consciousness follows after karma and life soul is from the death body and remains at the cemetery. Therefore if the cemetery is built in the right place then the life soul will increase and all the alive will be happy. Whereas bad cemetery decrease soul which bring unhappiness and often face illnesses. That is why cemetery is considered to be very important in Tibetan Sachey. It is said that when a corpse is placed in bad sachey. Even an animal can suffer the same.

Examining the sachey:

1) The way to examining favorable and unfavorable sky.

   According to the Geomancy Text, it is said that the father of Earth is Space, mother is Earth and the child is Space (bar nang). Therefore, before observing the Earth, one has to examine the sky first.

   Way of examining—Lie down in a prone (gyen gyal) position and examine the good and bad shape of the sky.

   Good: The sky should be like the mirror which is considered as the best, other shape like square, semicircle, white conch, swastika, lotus, like the belly of vase, like flying garuda are also one of the auspicious shape. So, when one sees the above shape will bring good result and happiness.

2) Method of finding good and bad back mountain of your house

3) Observing the right, left, infront and back

4) Favorable and unfavorable water

5) Good and bad path

6) Good and bad tree

7) Observing the favorable and unfavorable rock

8) Way of examine the four directions
9) Good and bad cemetery
10) Building the stupa
11) Hiding the treasure
12) Monastery and hermit
13) Observing the house
14) The year god and devil of 12 animal signs
15) Examining the foundation
16) Examine the good and bad of len

Few examples of good and bad sachey:
During the reign of King Songtsen Gampo, a temple (tsug lag khang). The result of sachey and the religious of Buddha had begun. King Trisong Deutsen requested to Bijey Tsenpa (Astrologer) to examine sachey when they are building the Samye Tsuglag Khang (Temple). He searched for the best geomancy and said:

Good Sachey:
"The hepo hill (a hill at a short distance from the grand monastery of Samye) is like the white conch lion jumping into the sky.
The mchims phu'i hill (near the great monastery of Samye) is like a turquoise lion leaping to the sky.
The Shar Ri (Eastern hill) is like the king sitting on a mattress.

The dge rgyas bye ma gling ri (near Samye), is like pile up precious.

The mchims phu'i valley is like an open lotus. The Red rocks like a coral lion bouncing up into the sky that pound is like a oil or butter slate. The southern river is like a turquoise green dragon walking upward.

The four mountain in Tibet which signify the progression of wealth, the "chobo" hill is like the pile up precious which signifies that continuity of saint may appear, some hill looks like vushang stone and skar chung which signify that people had enjoyed happily and live long life span, gzang gi ru lag birth-many intelligent minister will come, fight or conflicts may appear, the black mountain look like angry Mongolian etc. learnt all the sachey (earth observation) and could find the future happening. Great Master Padmasambhava invited; he had exorcised all the demons of Tibet on the way when was coming. He built a temple each on the bed sachey to eliminate it. Finally the Samye Temple had been built successfully and the king fulfilled his wishes.

Some few more examples of good Sachey are the Mahabodhi Stupa in Budhagaya, India, Bodh gaya where Buddha attained enlightenment. The Potala Palace in Lhasa, Tibet and the Forbidden City in Beijing are the most perfect examples of good geomancy. The durability of a building also depends mainly on Sachey.

Bad Sachey:

The son, Geden of Hor King suffered from Klu nad (disease caused by naga), since the King's palace was built on the place where naga resided. It is clear in the history of "*choes rje' sapen*" *book* and many other history books.

Nang Chey (House settings and observations):

Various consequences happen to all of us according to the changes of place. A house setting too very much affect the life of an individual's, economics, health, friendships, prosperity, peace, etc. House observation is a technique, which comes under geomancy, and plays a vital role in the life of an individual or family. Especially, the settings of fire stove, water tank, Main cupboard or Almirah, and the facing side of door are extremely important and should be observed. Failing to observe these major settings will bring disharmony within the family, ill-health, decline in wealth, emotional upsets etc. Therefore, settings and directions of the above four things are very much necessary and need consultation with an expert astrologer. Many times when there is a decline in family wealth and inauspicious things happen, changing and making necessary settings in the house will bring auspicious happenings. Generally it is important to apply the following four settings in one's house as instructed here:

Direction of Main Door: It should be best to face the main door at the East or South direction.

Direction of Fire Stove: The best direction to place the Gas stove in the kitchen is Westward.

Direction of Water tank or source: The side of water source or tap in the kitchen should be best place at the South direction.

Direction of Main cupboard: It should be place in the dark area where one stores ones main possessions or corner of a house. This cupboard refers to the shelf or utensil.

To be brief, by applying the knowledge of inner house observations and settings, one can transform the negative situation into a positive and constructive one. With this knowledge of geomancy, one can avoid harmful influences and obstacles, but can take the best advantage of environmental influences for general well being as well as to attain self-realization.

Glossary of Technical Terms

English	*Tibetan*
Natal chart/ horoscope	tses rab las rtsis
Life span	tshe tshad
Kalachakra	dus 'khor
Elemental astrology	'byung rtsis
Shiva Sarvodaya	dbyang 'char
Quotient	thob nor
Birth constellation	skyes skar
The nine Planets:	gza' dgu
i) Mars	mig mar
ii) Mercury	lhakpa
iii) Jupiter	phurbu
iv) Venus	pasang
v) Saturn	penpa
vi) The Sun	nyima
vii) The Moon	dawa
viii) Rahu	dachen gdong
ix) Ketu	dachen mjug
Sun sign	nyi khyim
Ascendant	tat kal
Marital Astrology	bag rtsis
Antidotes	gto chos
Yearly horoscope	keg rtsis

Illness Astrology		nad rtsis
Mount dwelling spirit		btsan
8 Goddesses calculation		lhamo rgyad rtsis
Death Astrology		gshin rtsis
Empty vase		bum stong
Astrologer's soul stone		rtsis pa'i bla rdo
The 5 disposal of corpse		dur sa lnga
Five elements		'byung ba lnga
The nature of the element		'byung ba'i ngo bo
Significance		nges tsigs
Classification		dbye ba
Characteristic		mtshan nyid
Function		byed las
Elemental relationship		ma, bu, da dok
12 animal sign		lo tak bcu bnyis
	i) Mouse	byi ba
	ii) Ox	glang
	iii) Tiger	stag
	iv) Rabbit	yos
	v) Dragon	sbrug
	vi) Snake	sbrul
	vii) Horse	rta
	viii) Sheep	lug
	ix) Monkey	sprel
	x) Bird	bya
	xi) Dog	khyi
	xii) Pig	phag

Changeable sign	log men
Life force	srog
Body/health	lus
Power	dbang
Luck	klung
Soul	bla
Soul day	bla gza
Life force day	srog gza
Foe day	gshed gza
Magic square number	sMeba
Life force magic number	srog sme
Body magic number	lus sme
Wealth magic number	dbang sme
Luck magic number	klung sme
I-ching	parkha
Birth I-ching	skyes spar
Changeable I-ching	babs spar
Constellations	rgyu skar
Twelve sectors of rise and fall	dar gud bcu gnyis
i) Conception	dbugs len
ii) Embryo	mngal gnas
iii) Foetus	lus rdzogs
iv) Birth	btsas pa
v) Ablution	'khrus byed
vi) Clothing	gos gyon
vii) Work	las byed
viii) Growth	dar ba

ix)	Decline	gud pa
x)	Ill-health	na ba
xi)	Death	shi ba
xii)	Cemetery	dur zhugs
Lord of the planets		bdag gza'
12 zodiac signs		khyim bcu gnyis
i)	Aries	lug
ii)	Taurus	glang
iii)	Gemini	'trig pa
iv)	Cancer	karta
v)	Leo	senge
vi)	Virgo	bumo
vii)	Libra	srang
viii)	Scorpio	sdig
ix)	Sagittarius	gzhu
x)	Capricorn	chu srin
xi)	Aquarius	bhumpa
xii)	Pisces	nya
Geomancy		sachey
Tomb-sign		dur mig
Multiple of nine		dbu mig
Bone element		rus khams
Eighty Sectors of the cemetery sign		dur gyi rkang pa brgyad bcu
Strong tomb sign		rang dur che
Weak tomb sign		rang dur chung

Strong adversarial tomb sign	gshed dur che
Weak adversarial tomb sign	gshed dur chung
Thirty six days of the tomb sign	dur gyi nyi ma so drug
Lesser constellation	skar chung
Heavenly door	snam sgo
Earthly door	sa sgo
Adversarial door	gshed sgo
Inner death wish	nang gi ro 'dod
Four looking eyes (the trigrams of the 4 cardinal directions)	lta ba'i mig bzhi
Four beating horns (the trigrams of the 4 corners directions)	brdung ra bzhi
Four Buddhist monk (The trigram li, kham, gin and zon)	ban bzhi
Four Bon priests (The trigram khen, khon, zin and da)	bon bzhi
The rotational magic square number	skor sme
Goat-horns (The dragon, sheep, dog and ox are designated as even-numbered signs)	
Rhino horns (tiger, snake, monkey and pig	ra ru

215

are designated as odd numbered signs)	
	bse ru
The greater and lesser outer death-wishes	
	phyi yi ro 'dod che chung
In auspicious years	lo ngan
The seven malign years	gdug pa can gyi lo bdun
The years endowed with two elements	'byung ba gnyis ldan lo
The years endowed with the five elements	'byung ba lnga ldan lo
Black fanged years	lo nag mche ba can
Heavenly lifeline	gnam gyi 'ju thag
Earthly peg	sa yi rtan phur
Cutting influence of demons	bdud chad
Roaming of the life spirit	bla 'khyam
Fourth removed adversarial year-sign	bzhi gshed
The thirty pairs of year-sign sharing a common body element	kha srog sum chu
Divine glory, life span and demon prognosis	lha dpal tshe bdud
Divine parentage	pha ma lha
Glorious offspring	bu tsha dpal
Harmonious life span	mthun pa tshe
Potent spirit	thub pa bdud

216

Impotent demon	mi thub bdud
Triple conjunction	gsum 'dom
Major planetary conjunction	gza' cheba
Lesser planetary conjunction	gza chung ba
Seven harsh factors	rtsub pa bdun
i) Obstacles to building	khang keg
ii) Obstacles to bedding	mal keg
iii) Environmental obstacles	yul keg
Opening keys	'byed pa'i lde mig
The Chinese method of pebble distribution	rgya nag rdel skor
Household sector	khang sa
Land sector	zhing sa
Cemetery sector	dur sa
Divination of the four pine-trees	thang shing bzhi
Divination of the fifteen golden bridges	gser zam bcho lnga
Divination of the branches of turquoise coloured juniper	gyu shug 'dab rgyas
Divination of the degree to which the grid is overstepped	ling tshe brgyal lam ma brgyal
Distinctive types of corpse	ro rigs dbye ba
Predictions concerning realms of subsequent rebirth	phyi ma'i skyes gnas
Predictions concerning the directions for corpse disposal	gshin po'i phung po gtong rim

The four favourable and	spar kha bzang
unfavourable trigram	bzhi ngan bzhi
i) Sky Medicine	gnam sman
ii) Life support	srog 'tsho
iii) Prosperity	dpal skyed
iv) Message of luck	phya lon
v) Harm	gnod pa
vi) Five Demons	'dre lnga
vii) Cutting influence of demons	bdud bcod
viii) Piece of body	lus chad

Bibliography

English Sources

1. Namkha'i Norbu, sgrung, lde'u and bon, (Narrations, Symbolic languages, and the Bon tradition in ancient Tibet), India: Dharamsala LTWA publication-1995.

2. Tai Situpa (the 12th), edited by Lea Terhune, Relative world, Ultimate mind, India: Penguin Books India-1999, printed at Chaman Offset printers, New Delhi.

3. Sherman Tai, Chinese Astrology, India: Sterling Publishers Pvt. Ltd.

4. Philippe Cornu, Tibetan Astrology, Shambhala Publication, Boston.

Tibetan Sources

1. Desi Sangye Gyatso, Baidurya Karpo, Tibet.

2. Xi-Tron press, Boe-kyi rtis-rig kun-due chenmo, Tibet.

3. Lochen Dharma Shri, 'byung rtsis man ngag zla ba'i 'od zer", Men-tesee khang, Dharamsala.

Reference Dictionaries

1. Tsepak Rigzin, Tibetan-English Dictionary of Tibetan Buddhist Terminology, LTWA, Dharamsala.
2. Dr. Tsering Thakchoe Drungtso, Tibetan-English Dictionary of Tibetan Medicine and Astrology, India: Dharamsala-Drungtso publication-1999.
3. Sarat Chandra Das, A Tibetan-English Dictionary, Sri Satguru publications, India.
4. Acharya Karma Monlam, The New English-Tibetan Dictionary, Dept. of Education, Dharamsala.

TARA TIBETAN ASTROLOGICAL SERVICE

(Ancient Tibetan Wisdom to lighten our path of progress and guide our future)

Tara Tibetan Astrology is a nonsectarian platform for presentation of courses on Tibetan Astrology and related subjects. It is perhaps the first in the world to offer three months basic and advance correspondence courses on Tibetan Astrology via email. The aim of the course is to generate awareness about Tibetan Astrology, provide a foundation for the student to become a professional Tibetan Astrologer, and to preserve and promote the Tibetan Astrology in the world community. Certification for the course is given to students who answer all questions satisfactorily at the end of each course. Tibetan Astrology is a comprehensive and powerful tool, which provides a right guidance in everyone's daily life. Tara Tibetan Astrology also offers seminars, workshops, teachings, consultations, marital chart, medical chart, yearly predictions, general and special protective amulets, and full Life written horoscope of past, present and future by using planetary calculations and an elemental horoscope together with the Arising Vowels system.

Jung Tsee Astrology of the Elements

Jung Tsee traditional Tibetan system of Astrology is believed to be taught by Manjushri, the lord of wisdom and is based on the calendar cycles of Elements, Animal signs, Trigrams, Nine magic square numbers and their cycles and effects in our lives. These understandings will enable one to calculate and interpret the Elemental Horoscope for any person. This comprehensive course gives insight into the character of Life Force, Health, Economic, Fortune, Power, Capacity, Compatibility, as well as a variety of other results, including interpretation of the changing effects during the cycles of years. The Medical chart **(Ney-Tsee)**, s Tibetan Geomancy **(Sachey),** and Death calculation **(Shin-Tsee)** all comes under Elemental Astrology and interpreted according to the context of Moon Rays Text of Elemental Astrology **(Jung—Tsee Zla-b'i Od-Zer).**

Kar Tsee—Astronomy

Kar Tsee is also known as Kalachakra Astrology and is based upon the stars, constellations, and planets. The External Kalachakra **(Chi Dhue Kyi Khor-lo)**, focuses on the creation of universe, it's cosmology, the movements of the planets and stars. The Internal Kalachakra **(Nang Dhue Kyi Khor-lo),** provides an understanding on the three fundamental interdependent components of our body Viz: Energy Channels **(Tsa),** Wind **(Loong),** Essential Drops **(Thig ley),** and the effect that external forces such as planets and stars have on our body. Kalachakra Astrology explained that the energy Channels are like our home, essential drops as our property and energy wind and mind as the owner. Where as the Secret Kalachakra Astrology **(Sang wa Dhue kyi Khorlo)** emphasis on the subject of meditation, Spiritual exercises, initiations, power and visualization of one's own personal deity **(Yidam)**. The word Kalachakra means " Wheel of Time", which refers to the unique presentation of cycles of time within the Kalachakra Tantra. By understanding this vast subject one can used it for self-development, to lead a healthy life and can draw the Life horoscope of self and others.

dByangs-'char-Arising Vowel

Yangcher astrology, is a very secret teaching which was first taught by the Hindu Lord Shiva (Tib. dBang-phyug-Chenpo). This system of Astrology is assumed to have come into Tibet together with the Buddhism. Although this text had been translated into Tibet quite early, it had not been widely used and remained concealed in the knowledge of only few people. The Root text of Arising Vowel, having ten chapters was translated into Tibetan literature from the original Sanskrit text by the famous

translator Sherab Rinchen in the 12th century A.D. The
ten major chapters are about Zhi-rGyas dBang-drag
(Peaceful, Progressive, Powerful and Violent activities).
It presents the cycles of the universe in terms of the
sequences of transforming sounds through the months
and days of the year. Yangcher or Arising vowel astrology
calculations are mainly based upon the appearance of
letters, to which numbers are attributed, in a sentence
related to the fact under prognostication. There are also
over hundreds of Circular diagrams (Tib. 'khor-lo) in
Arising Vowel astrology which can be drawn for different
events like determining the yearly events of any kingdom
or nation with respect to weather, agriculture, wars,
relations with , other nations etc., as well as personal
prognostication in terms of one's health, wealth,
relationship and property. .

Sa Chey—Tibetan Geomancy

Sa Chey or science of Earth observation dates back at
least 3000 years. Its philosophies and symbols have their
origins in an earlier period of Tibetan History back to
Zhang zhung and Bon era. Tibetan Geomancy emphasis
looking at surrounding while building a house, temple,
monastery, palace, stupa and even cemetery etc. Samye
Temple is one typical example, which was built in 781,
Iron Ox year according to Tibetan Geomancy. The

happiness and unhappiness, success and unsuccessful, prosperity and misfortune all mostly depend upon the good or bad Geomancy.

The house settings also plays a very important role which affect the situation of an individual or family life with respect to economic, health, friendship, prosperity, peace, success etc. Therefore, settings and directions of main door, fire stove, main cupboard and water tank or tape are especially important and needed consultation with the expert Geomancer or Astrologer. By applying the knowledge of outer house observations and inner settings, one can transform the negative situation into a positive and constructive one. Thus, by knowing Tibetan Geomancy, one can avoid harmful influences and obstacles and can take the best advantage of environmental influences for general well being as well as to attain self-realization.

Ney Tsee—Medical Astrology

Medical Astrology is prepared in many ways according to reliable ancient sources. The Eight Goddess Calculation (Lhamo Gey Tsee), Seven Week days Divination scripture (Za Doon Mo Pey) and many other means. It is mainly prepared and drawn for those patients who had prolong medication and least improvement in their health condition. The Medical astrologer gives the antidotes and rituals and guides per the astrological calculation and divination. Through astrological calculation shows the right physician to consult and many a times identify harming spirits. The internal Kalachakra and Tibetan medical texts share many similarities regarding the mode of treatment, remedial measures, rites and rituals, medicines, behavioural guidelines, yogic practice etc. Both the astrological and medical texts emphasizes and hold the same view, regarding the formation of human body, disease as an expression of imbalance among those elements and the corresponding treatment which should be composed by the same elemental substances.

Individual Horoscope interpretation

The astrological assessment and interpretation of prediction guides all aspects of an individual's daily life from health to enlightenment. It also helps people know their stars, accept their karma and prepare themselves in a more positive manner from a bright future. This chart is drawn as per the age-old traditional text and serves as a lamp, which helps to vanquish all the darkness caused by the ignorance. The chart explains about one's past, future and present life condition with respect to health, economic, relationship, children, job, good and bad days etc. For accurate and detailed chart one's personal Date of birth, time of birth, place of birth and gender are necessary.

Tibetan Astrological Amulet

General and special amulets for health, wealth, luck, love, wisdom, peace, concentration, balance of mind, career, life force, marriage, child related problems etc., based upon a person's Tibetan horoscope are also available by direct order from Tsering Dolma Drungtso.

-Wear on the body or keep with personal items
-Hang above the entry door to a home or room
-Use in a car or whilst traveling.

Future Plan of Tara Tibetan astrology Service Centre

Tara Tibetan astrology Service Centre or consultancy is dedicated to providing its clients with authentic Tibetan astrological services and aims to promote traditional Tibetan astrology to the world. This centre is initiating and working on some translations of Tibetan Astrology with the mere aim of providing high quality courses on Tibetan Astrology. With this humble motivation we have already translated the essence of most important elemental text " Moon Rays Oral Instruction Elemental" (Tib. byung rTsis Man-nag Zla-b'i Od-zer) in this book. We have also listed and plan to translate some key texts and commentary in the near future. Despite our best trial and perseverance with humble motivation in this project, we still fear when we will be able to present some of the demanding rich treasures of the many aspects and varieties of Tibetan astrology to our interested astrologers, scholars and lay person.

With such a vastness of the subject matter, this project is obviously not likely to be completed overnight. For this we need the hands of astrologers and translators who have very solid backgrounds in the astrological sciences and its related subjects. Currently, this project is being funded entirely by the Drungtso Tibetan Healing and Astrological Service Centre, Dharamsla, India. We are willing to undertake joint research and project on the subject, if any one comes with sincere idea and financial support.

In order to make available the rich wisdom of ancient Tibetan astrology into the English-speaking world, contributions, financial or otherwise, to this project are most welcome. Contributors or supporters will receive regular reports on the progress of this project, a copy of each book printed, as well as a 15% discount on any of the services provided by this centre like courses, consultation etc.

Mode of Payment:

Please make payment either through International Money order, Bank cheque or Western Union Money Transfer in the name of Mrs. Tsering Dolma Drungtso. The astrological work will start only after advance payment is done.

Tsering Dolma Drungtso can be reached at:

e-mail: tibastro@yahoo.com
        drdrungtso@yahoo.com
        tsedoldrung@hotmail.com
Phone: 091-1892-28034
Handy: 98170 92550

Excerpts from Letters Send to the Author

"Thank you very much for the horoscope. I enjoyed reading it and hope that it will be a good guide for my living years. My character is very close to that one, that you read out of the stars."

—Uli Paulus
Nernberg, GERMANY

"Thank you so much for your assistance! I received the astrology chart the other day, and its news made me so happy."

—Bridget A. Llanes
Vancouver, CANADA

"Since I began wearing your amulet my health has improved quit fast. I am now spending a lot of time-out of bed though I cannot walk very far yet. Thank you a million times!"

—Colin Graham
Dorset, ENGLAND

"Thank you for completing my horoscope reading. Almost all of the reading is very true and accurate."
—Sandra Lee Tatum
Santa Fe, USA

"Thank you for my chart. You will be happy to know that all the events you mentioned in my earlier years match up!"

—Krissy Picoli
Queensland, AUSTRALIA

"I bet soon you will be the most known internationally Tibetan astrologer. Tibetan culture is getting very popular in the West, especially in European countries. So the first people who would be able to introduce the subject are very important. I wish you a lot of inspiration on this way and a lot of professional success! Thank you so much for the beginners course and I would like to continue with the advance course."

—Gilles Deniau
Venezia, ITALY

"I appreciate your wonderful message to me. I will make an effort to do my best in the future."
—Tomoyuki Yamashita
Shimoda City, JAPAN

"I was recommended by a friend and she spoke very highly of you. I would like for you to give me a reading."
—Francine Putnam
THAILAND

" There are many astrologer on the world and I also have friends in France, but I always heard that Tibetan Astrology was very good, and I have also been told by Christopher (whom you did chart) that what you told him was very relevant. I therefore told myself that I should not loose contact with you."
—Alexandre Neol-
Paris, FRANCE

Author offering a traditional scarf to all the Tibetan Astrology seminar participants on the closing ceremony (29th January, 2001), which was held at Maitripa Contemplative Centre, Melbourne, AUSTRALIA